Management Guru
Chãnakya
Stategaft and His Policies

Prof. Shrikant Prasoon

V&S PUBLISHERS

Published by:

V&S PUBLISHERS

F-2/16, Ansari Road, Daryaganj, New Delhi-110002
☎ 011-23240026, 011-23240027 • *Fax:* 011-23240028
Email: info@vspublishers.com • *Website:* www.vspublishers.com

Regional Office : Hyderabad
5-1-707/1, Brij Bhawan (Beside Central Bank of India Lane)
Bank Street, Koti, Hyderabad - 500 095
☎ 040-24737290
E-mail: vspublishershyd@gmail.com

Branch Office : Mumbai
Jaywant Industrial Estate, 2nd Floor-222, Tardeo Road
Opposite Sobo Central, Mumbai - 400 034
☎ 022-23510736
E-mail: vspublishersmum@gmail.com

Follow us on:

All books available at **www.vspublishers.com**

© **Copyright:** V&S PUBLISHERS
Edition 2017

Publisher's Note

V&S Publishers has chosen to simplify subjects or works that readers find difficult to understand. One such subject being simplified here is the man Chanakya and his governance doctrines explained in the Arthashastra. . Although this book is ostensibly authored by Kautilya, most scholars agree that Kautilya was a pen name of Chanakya. Chanakya was the minister to Chandragupta Maurya, the founder of the Mauryan Empire, which emerged in an environment when India was under attack from the northern area. Chanakya was said to have played a leading role in assembling and administering this large empire. In the Arthashastra, he compiles his observations of statecraft based on this experience.

This book is a prescriptive text that lays out rules and norms for successfully running a state and conducting international relations. The original book abounds in generalities and is not descriptive of specific, historical events or battles. In this way, he sought to make the text useful and relevant in a variety of situations, across eras. It also lays out general rules for a variety of subjects, such as architecture, alchemy, astronomy, and pleasure. The term Arthashastra itself means rules or norms of artha, a concept translated as "means of life" or "worldly success." Like the book 'The Prince' by Machiavelli, then, Arthashastra is a guide for rulers on how to successfully govern a state -a sort of "Textbook for Kings."

V&S Publishers hope the readers would appreciate the man named Chanakya and his pragmatic qualities.

Dedication

Dedicated to All
Who Wish and Try to Manage:
Self; Family; Society
And their Organization
For Greater Gain
And Higher Attainment

Contents

Introduction

Chānakya thought on all related branches and boughs of management keeping a really big empire at the centre for focus. He thought for all; for the benefit, survival and prosperity of all; so this book is for all: Writers, Thinkers, Managers, Politicians, Human Resource Personnel, Military Personnel, Traders, Management Trainers, Management Consultants, Management Trainees, Management Students, Government Officials and General Readers.

In this book I have tried to write Chānakya's biography; his achievements and accomplishments and his ideas about accumulating wealth, establishing, managing and ruling an empire. I have done the best that was possible.

Now, it is up you, the readers, to judge whether I have been able to present and reveal the real Chãnakya or not; whether his relation with management is established well or not; whether ancient management is described in detail with reference to modern management or not, and whether I have given everything that you need for growth and prosperity or not. It will be a real pleasure if the readers get a lot more than their expectation.

Only "ā" has been taken from scriptural Transliteration for the long "a" sound, which is otherwise impossible to write in the Roman script. Rest everything is as written in government papers, magazines, newspapers and general books. It will help the readers read the few Mantras and many *Sutras* and Shlokas quoted in it.

Sarve Shubhe!

Prof. Shrikant Prasoon

1

Meaning of Artha, Economy

Chānakya was a shrewd observer of nature, human beings and non-human beings. He had an uncanny ability to co-relate many things wisely to come to a solid and true conclusion. It opened his inner eyes, gave him powerful insight and made him a thoughtful theoretician. This showed others the ways to be followed and means to be adopted not only during his lifetime but till today through his aphorisms and dictums. A seemingly insignificant sight will be sufficient to explain this.

Once the Mauryan forces had to hide in a cave. They were defeated and chased by the big and powerful Magadh Army. There was no food, and the soldiers were starving. They could not come out of the cave either, as there was a threat to their lives. The Magadh Army was still very close to them.

Chānakya saw an ant taking a grain of rice, even though there was no sign of food or grains anywhere. Moreover, the rice grain was cooked. He took that grain. It was freshly cooked and still soft. He ordered the soldiers to search and they found that their enemies had been dining behind the cave. Indeed, they were eating at the ground and were not prepared for a war. They must have been coming there in large groups to take their meal with their weapons collected at different places. As soon as they saw the Mauryans, they escaped leaving behind the weapons, horses, chariots and food to last for weeks. Hungry young Mauryans chased them without engaging in actual battle. They got food and weapons that they needed the most and thus were saved.

Appraisal

To be conscious towards every movement and events taking place all around gives unfathomable inner strength. It takes time, practise and concentration to achieve that rare quality. A person with that ability keeps an eye on everything; overlooks nothing and is never deceived.

Effect

Nothing that happens is meaningless because each incident has a cause behind and at the beginning.

Rights, Duties and Responsibilities of the Governing Body

The *Kautilya Arthashāstra* is not about a subject called Economics that is taught and learnt in schools and colleges. It includes all sorts of disciplined and moral, legal and ethical earnings. It fixes the ways and rules of earning. It does not provide the study of economy in theory; or of the study of the economy of a particular country or section in particular. It is neither theoretical nor practical economics. Moreover, it fixes the ways and means of earning and fulfilling responsibilities towards the governing body including the rights, duties and responsibilities of the governing body or the king.

At the end of the book in the concluding *Prakaran* or chapter, Kautilya declares the meaning of *artha*:

Manushyānām vrittih arthah: the livelihood of human beings is called *artha*.

Manushyavati bhumih iti arthah: the land occupied by human beings is called *artha*.

Tasyāh prithivyā lābha pālana upāyah shāstram artha shāstram iti: The science that discusses and shows ways and means for the procurement and safe use or safety of such lands is called *Arthashāstra*.

In India, this science has been given a very wide scope. It gives ideal teaching that: *Dharma artha virodhena kāmam seveta na nihsukhah syāt*: One should follow the dictates of *dharma* and *artha*. One who moves in the opposite direction is never happy.

➤ To pray for someone in meek words: *tvāmi mam artham arthayate*;

➤ To try to get something: *priyā pravritti nimittam abhyartaye*;

➤ Meaning, cause, purpose, wish, desire: *gyān arthogyān sambandhah shrotum shrotah*.

There are three types of meanings

(a) *vāchya, abhivyakt* or *abhidhā* (simple, general)

(b) *lakshya, lakshanā* (symbolic, intentional);

(c) *vyangya* (ironical, satirical)

➤ Cause, reason, means, that which can be perceived by senses (*roop, rasa, gandh, sparsh, shabda*) *indriyabhyah parāhya arthā arthe bhyashcha param manah*

➤ Proceedings, business, proposal, work (*artho ayam arthāntar bhāvya yeva*)

> Wealth, money, worldly accumulations, one of the pursuits (*apya arth kāmau tasya āstām dharma yeva manishinah*)

> Use, welfare, profit, wholesome deeds (*tathā hi sarve tasya āsan parārthe kaphalā gunāh*)

> Way, type, technique

> To stop; to keep away; annihilate

Arth āgam, accumulation of wealth or receiving money is pleasant; *arth upārjanam*, earning money is essential for sustenance; though the people have lost *arth gauravam*. It is the reality, *Arth tattvam*. *Arth dushanam*, extravagant expenditure, must be stopped for balanced living for a long time. Some such people try to evade and search for some substitute or *arth vikalp*.

Chānakya in the *Kautilya Arthshāstram* has given 32 types of *arth*, meanings. It is very interesting to see them. In the wake of popularizing English words we are going far away from such meaningful words. It must be read carefully, all the three: *shabda, sutra* and *arth*. Chānkya says that the livelihood of human beings is called artha; the land inhabited by men is also called artha; and the branch of study that deals with acquiring land, controling it, and keeping it in control is called *Arthshāstra*. That the *Arthshāstra* follows 32 ways to acquire control and manage it. The following are Kautilya's or Chānakya's way of accumulating and managing wealth. In it he is the first management guru that has dealt with the topic in detail and has given the general and uncanny ways for the benefit of all human beings. They are the following:

1. **Adhikaran**: *yama artham adhikritya uchyate tad adhikaranam*; whatever is said authoritatively is called *adhikaran*.

2. **Vidhānam**: sh*āstra prakaran anupurvi vidhānam*; to speak according to the situation is called *Vidhān*.

3. **Yogah**: *vākya yojanā yogah*; the construction of a sentence is called yoga; *chatur varnāshramo lokah*.

4. **Padārth:** *padāva adhikah padārthah*; only the meaning of a word is called *padārth*.

5. **Hetvarthah:** *hetuk arth sādhako hetvarthah*, that which proves the meaning, for example: *arth mulau hi dharma kāmau*; religion and sex depend on wealth.

6. **Uddeshah:** *samās vākyam uddeshah*; the statement in a short sentence is called *Uddesh* or purpose, for example, *vidyā vinay hetruh indriya jayah*, learning and humility depends on the control of senses.

7. **Nirdeshah:** *vyās vākyam nirdeshah*, the statement describing a thing in detail is called direction, *nirdesh*.

8. **Upadeshah:** The statement that tells how to behave is called *Upadesh*. For example: one should work according to the scriptures and available finance.

9. **Apadeshah:** *Yevam sāvāhetu apadeshah*, when the statement of another person is quoted, it is called *Apadesh*.

10. **Atideshah:** *Iuktena sādhanam Atideshah*, to prove what is not said with what has been said is called *Atidesh*.

11. **Pradeshah:** *Ivyaktavyena sādhanam Pradeshah*, to prove what is said with what is to be said is called *Pradesh*.

12. **Upamānam:** *Drishtena ādrishtasya sādhanam Upamānam*, to prove the unseen with the seen things is called *Upamāna*.

13. **Arthāpati:** *Yada anukatam arthād āpyate sa Arthapatih*, that which is gained from the unsaid things is called *Arthāpati*.

14. **Sanshayah:** *Ubhayato hetum anarthah sanshayah*, when a thing appears the same to the opposite parties, it is called *Sanshaya*.

15. **Prasangah:** *Prakarnantarena samān arthah Prasangah*; the similarity of meaning with another event is called *Prasang*.

16. **Viparyaya:** *Pratilomena sādhanam viparyayah,* to indicate a thing with opposite statements is called *Viparyaya.*

17. **Vākya Sheshah:** *Yena vākyam samāpyate, sa vākya sheshah,* the closing of a sentence is called *Vākya Shesh.*

18. **Anumatam:** *Par vākyam prati siddham Anumatam,* the statement by another person which has not been opposed is called *Anumatam.*

19. **Vyākhyānam:** *Atishaya varnanā Vyākhyānam,* to prove in different ways, what has already been proved is called *Vyākhyāna.*

20. **Nirvachanam:** *Gunatah shabda nishpatih nirvachanam,* to prove something by giving meaning is called *Nirvachanam.*

21. **Nidarshanam:** *Drishtānto drishtānta yukto Nidarshanam,* to clarify something with examples is called *Nidarshanam.*

22. **Apavargah:** *Abhipluta vyapakarshanam Apavargah,* to discuss the rules so much in detail that it dimnishes the subject, is called *Apavargah.*

23. **Swa-sangyā:** *Paraira sanmitah shabdah swa-sangyāI,* the word that is used without any directive from others is called *swa-sangyā.*

24. **Purva Pakshah:** *Pratishedhvyam vākyam purva pakshah;* the sentence that admonishes is called *Purva Paksha.*

25. **Uttar Pakshah:** *Tasya nirnayan vākyam uttar paksham;* that which denies the statement of *Purva Paksha* is called *Uttar Paksha.*

26. **Ekāntah:** *Sarva trāyatam Ekāntah;* that statement which can't be left out at any place or any time, is called *Ekāntah.*

27. **Anāgat Āvekshanam:** *Panchādevam vihitam itya Anāgat Āvekshanam,* the provision that has to be made in the future is called *Anāgat Āvekshanam.*

28. **Atikrānta Āvekshanam**: *Purastād yevam vihitam itya Atikrānta Āvekshanam*; the provision that has already been made is called *Pratikrānta Āvekshanam*.

29. **Niyogah**: *Yevam nānyath iti Niyogah*, the statement that says that this work is to be performed in this way or not at all, is called *Niyoga*.

30. **Vikalpah**: *Anena vānena veti Vikalpah*; the thing can be done either this way or that way, is called *Vikalpa*.

31. **Samuchchyah**: *Anena cha anena cha iti samuchchyah*; a thing that can be done in this way and that way, is called *Samuchchya*.

32. **Uhyam**: *Anukta karanam Uhyam*; to do what has not been said, is called *Uhya*.

In this way, Arth has 32 divisions and the *Artha Shāstram* by Kautilya deals with all these 32 ways and means:

Yevam shāstram idam yuktam yetābhih tantra yukti bhih;
Avāptau pālane cha uktam lokasyāsya parasya cha.

This Artha (and Arthshāstra) encourages one to indulge in Artha and Kāma, save them, and destroy opposition caused by non-religious activities:

Dharmam artham cha kāmam cha pravartayati pāti cha;
Adharma anarth vidveshān idam shāstram idam nihanti cha.

In the concluding lines (180th *Prakaran*) it is said that this Arthshāstra is written by that Vishnugupta Kautilya, who freed the land, weapons and scriptures from King Nand:

Yena shāstram cha shastram cha nand rāja gatā cha bhuh;
Amarshena udhritānya āshu tena shāstram idam kritam.

When *artha* is to be taken as one of the pursuits then it cannot be taken in its limited connotation, and only as the money or the wealth. As pursuit it must cover all. Moreover, mere accumulation of money is not *artha*; its best and most advantageous utilization is also allied with it. Money must be *ānand dāyakam; dharma dhārakam* and *Moksha kārkam:* money must give pleasure; keep morality intact and be a provision for liberation. If otherwise, then money is useless. We know, only a single way to use money: to buy things for food and luxury. This is not utilization at all, it is spending, expense. One must take it in its widest perspective.

Due to the broad attitude that Chānakya perceived and followed, he was successful in fulfilling his higher and almost unachievable dreams.

2

Destroying Old Order and Enemies

Uproot which Pinches

One famous incident from Chānakya's life proves how strong, inimical, intolerant he was; and how he yearned for the safety and obstacle-free path towards the goal. Perhaps he believed in demolishing dilapidated structure and old order for greater gain, better creation and smooth progress.

One day a kush (a kind of grass, with a sharp needle-like top, used in the religious observances by the Hindus) pricked Chanak's foot, the father of Chānakya. It became septic and eventually Chanak died. Chānkya did observe the rituals but he could neither forget nor forgive kush. He studied it, made preparations and started uprooting and annihilating the very species of kush by pouring whey at the broken roots of kush so that they may not germinate or grow again. This was his way of showing anger and taking vengeance.

The people were amazed to see it. A young man taking whey every morning and going out in search of kush, uprooting them and pouring at each root, a bit of whey to erase them was a sight to watch. Some of them didn't like it. They protested. It had no effect on the mind and action of the revengeful and determined Chānakya. One day, some elderly persons (In another version, one of the ministers of Nand, saw him uprooting kush and the brilliance on his face,) went to Chānakya who was busy in uprooting and destroying quite innocent looking but sharp needle-like kush. They politely asked, ``What and why are you doing?''

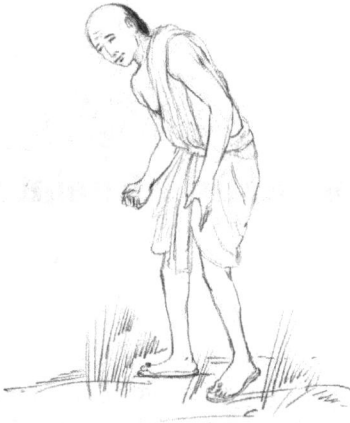

"I'm uprooting and destroying this pinching kush because I can't tolerate anything against man or humanity, and whosoever goes against man or humanity I'll destroy it."

He was true to his word. His body language expressed more than his words. The minister thought him to be the best person to go against Nand and destroy him. It was that Minister who invited him to a feast arranged by the king knowing well that Nand will not tolerate a black brāhmin and this brāhmin won't tolerate Nand. It will suit him. That way, Chānakya reached the palace.

He won't easily express his mind for he held the view one should not make their inner decisions known to others. He said, "manasā vichintyayet vachasā na prakāshayet."

At some places it's written that once he was going to some place with his disciples. He had taken an un-treaded route. He wore no protection for his feet. A kush pricked. It was painful. He immediately asked the pupils to bring whey, to uproot them and to pour whey at each root to abolish it completely. When other men asked him the reason of his anger he plainly replied that he can't tolerate any obstacle on his way. He further added that he liked to uproot whatever pinched.

Appraisal

It is almost impossible to ascend higher without creating enemies, and doubly difficult to ascend higher in the face of the enemies. Face the enemies wisely and at the right opportunity without losing a lot of time, energy or resources.

The Vow: Resolution and Aim

There are different versions of each incident associated with Chānakya. The writers have used their own imagination to paint the person, visualize his moves and express his ideas. This one is not an exception. Usually, it is said that Chānakya went to the court of Magadhnaresh Ghanānand on his own but another version says that because he was a scholar he was made the president of a charitable trust and met the king for the first time as the president of the said trust. But it can't be true that all such appointments were made directly by the king.

The most convincing tale is that he was invited by one of the ministers to attend a feast arranged by the king and when Nand saw him, he was angry and asked his men to throw the black brāhmin out of the court. This insult was such that Chānakya was too angry to be checked and took a vow to destroy the king and his clan.

There is yet another version that one minister from the court of the Magadhnaresh who was angry with him as he was insulted by the king, took Chānakya to the court. He knew something about Chānakya's background, power, and nature. He invited him to the court knowing well that the king will not tolerate his black face and arrogant ways. He will insult the Brāhmin and the Brāhmin will take the revenge. His aim will be fulfilled. He did exactly as he planned and truly enough, the luxuriant king forgot the courtesy to be shown towards a Brāhmin. Whatever the reason, Chānakya was in the court of King Ghanānand.

On the other hand Nand laughed at the black and ugly Brāhmin:

"Is he a Brāhmin? A Brāhmin can't be black and if black he can't be a Brāhmin." It had dual meanings.

Chānakya did not like the ways of the king. He protested but of no avail. The minister concerned was pleased with the expected turn in event. He sided with his king which angered Chānakya even more. The situation grew tense.

Many of them didn't like to insult a Brāhmin but Ghanānand was obstinate. He won't listen to reason. He loved luxury and was cruel to the people. He had brutally taxed the people to fill the treasure. People were annoyed. He was not popular among them. It was because of his temperament, character and behaviour.

Ghanānand started laughing at the Brāhmin who was fast losing his patience. He roared in the court against the king. In return the king ordered:

"Throw this Brāhmin out of the court."

It brought the end of the preserved patience. Chānkya broke loose. He showered verbal curses on the king and the kingdom. No one was

able to check them. In a fit of anger Ghanānand inflicted more injury. The angry Brāhmin freed himself from the grip of the soldiers, untied the sacred lock of hair at the crown of the head, and took a vow:

"Ghanānand, I have come to show you the true path and stop you from luxurious living, free you from surā and sunderi, wine and women, but you won't listen to reason. I take a vow in the presence of all that I will annihilate you and your dynasty. I won't take rest till you are not destroyed along with your posterity. I will not bind my choti (the lock of hair) till you are not uprooted."

Chānakya marched out of the court in that angry mood.

Appraisal

Don't make a promise but in case you make a promise then fulfill it in time and with the best ability. Don't take a vow but in case you take a vow then direct all your energy and resources to make your vow come true. That gives immense confidence and pleasure of being a winner.

Effect

We grow from inside. Our power comes from inside. The inner soul is all "energy". Enrich it for instant and greater success.

The Preparations

The king was not worried. After all, what could a feeble Brāhmin do to him? But Chānakya was restless. He could not forget the vow taken in the court, in the presence of the courtiers. His open lock of hair reminded him many times everyday rather whenever he touched it or whenever the air blew it. He had taken such a great vow which was obviously very difficult to fulfill. He lost his appetite, his sleep. He stopped thinking about anything else.

He had to arrange each and everything, from a simple needle to a sharp and heavy sword. This made him a tireless worker, busy almost the whole day and whole night and in-between taking a nap here and an hour's sleep there.

Establishing an Empire or Organization

Chānakya showed us the way how to get a vow come true by exterminating the Nanda Dynasty, who were the rulers of the Magadha Empire. The entire dynasty became traceless. It was a grand success for Chānakya. It is the only example of a strong empire being uprooted by an individual who had neither wealth nor army; neither a house nor a living; neither land nor residence; neither known people nor known resources; and neither weapons nor physical strength. That is why Chānakya declares that knowledge and wisdom is everything to get success.

The Birth of Arthashāstra

Though, the legendary work *Kautilya Arthashāstra* was written very late but Chānakya conceived the idea of the work while thinking about the infamous Magadha King Ghanānand and comparing him with a great and righteous king. It got its roots in his mind when he was planning the demolition of the Nand dynasty, and construction of a new empire, making preparations, acquiring material wealth, gaining in strength, raising an army, and training recruits. At that time he had both the ideas of destruction and construction running parallel in his mind.

He declared that the learned king who works for the welfare of all living beings and is always ready to do the best for the administration and education of the people rules over his kingdom for a long time:

Vidyā vinito rājā hi prajānām vinaye ratah;
Ananyām prithivim bhungagkte sarva bhuta hite ratah.

Vriddha Sanyogah

He can win any land and rule for a long time if one had won over the six enemies – sex, anger, lust, ego, pride, and jealousy (*kāma- krodha- lobha- mān- mad- aharsha tyāgāt kāryah*).

A king can't do anything singnificant as one wheel will not move the chariot. So, many helping hands are needed, *Sahāya asādhyam rājatvam chakram yekam na vartate.* For that purpose different persons suited for different jobs are to be appointed.

The *Arthashāstra* classifies legal matters into civil and criminal and it specifies elaborate guidelines for administering justice in terms of evidence, procedures and witnesses. Furthermore, Kautilya strongly believed in *Dandniti*, though he maintained that penalties must be fair and just, and proportionate to the offence committed. The people don't like the king who announces disproportionate tough punishments; they don't obey a lenient king, so it is better to give just and proportionate punishment,

Teekshna dando hi bhutānām udejaniya.
Mridu dandah paribhuyate.
Yathārtha dandah pujyah.

Vārtā- Danda- Niti- Sthāpanā

In *Arthashāstra*, 6000 verses, mainly prose with about 380 *shlokas*, have been divided into 15 *adhikaranas* (books) and 150 *adhyāyas* and 180 *prakaranas* (sections dealing with one topic). It begins with *Mulāni*-Foundations and *Mantrinah*-Counselors

In short it can be seen in this way:

Kāryam – Work	*Mantrinah-Kāryarthi-*
Rājya Tantram - Mangement	*Mantra*-Policies, Strategies
Kārya Siddhih – Work Accomplished	*Kāryārthi* – Work manager
	Juga Loka – Human relations
Rājya Neeti – Management Science	*Sandhi* – Alliances
	Arthakamau – Wealth and Desires
Sāhas – Managerial Actions	*Danda* - Enforcement
Ācharanam – Behaviour	*Charitram* – Character
Artha – Resources	*Utsāh* – Enthusisam,
Dosha – Faults	Entrepreneurship
Kāryavyāpti – Working	*Svajana* – Own people
Dharma – Ethics	

The Basic Factors

Kingdom or organization or an enterprise is the basis of resources. One person can earn enough but only for a family but if hundreds, or thousands or lakhs of people are working for a person who owns a kingdom or an enterprise then the profit earned by all the men after deducting their salary adds up to the resources of that man and hence, his earning multiplies hundreds of times. The resources are controlled, surplus generated and used for different purposes through the possession of a kingdom. Chānakya draws attention towards certain facts. The large nations states/ corporations today are similar in structure to kingdoms but are governed by elected/appointed representatives of the people/ stakeholders. The development of science, technology and engineering with the market economy has resulted in wealth generation through the industry and services sector. This is in addition to agriculture which has always existed.

The basis of enterprise is rooted in conquering the body organs

> Management of "everything" begins with management of "self".

24

- Management cannot be separated from the manager.

- *Indriya* or organs of sense – eyes, ears, nose, tongue, and skin.

- Organs of action: Hands, feet, mouth, reproduction, and excretion.

- Organ of perception: Mind

- Manifestation of *indriya jaya*: Control over: *kāma, krodha, lobha, moha, mada* and *matsarya.*

- *Indriyajayasya mulam vinayam*: The conquest of the organs lies in training/discipline.

- Mastery of the self lies in the self; discipline/humility generated by training in ethics.

- *Virupasevanam vigyānam*: Worldly knowledge is learned from serving the elders.

- *Vigyānam*: Sciences and art; human behaviour.

- *Gyānam*: Spiritual/philosophical knowledge.

- *Vijnanaena atmamanam sampādyet*: Equip yourself fully with worldly knowledge; enrich yourself internally; cognitive acquisition of worldly knowledge followed by internalization leading to appropriate behaviour, in practise lead to better performance at tasks undertaken.

- *Sampaditātma jitātma bhavati*: One who has acquired knowledge is the one who has conquered himself. Totally self-controlled professional leader/manager acts in the long-term interest of the organization; resists acting in self interest which conflicts with organizational interest; does not succumb to pressure of immediate interests against long-term interests; resists temptations to do good to the organization at the cost of society, nations and stakeholders; prepared to quit rather make decisions against convictions.

➤ *Jitātmā Sarvarthe sanyujyate*: The self-conquered should endow himself with all resources.

➤ *Sarvarthe*: All resources: Men; Money; Materials; Methods.

❦

3

The Last Blow

After worldly knowledge is acquired, resources do not come on their own. They have to be deliberately acquired in order to be victorious in all tasks undertaken and enterprise building. These are parts of the preparation for the final blow to the opposition and for blowing the victory bugle.

From day one, Chānakya kept on thinking and planning the final blow to Nand dynasty. He rescheduled his plans and started attacking the border areas where the king would take time to reach, giving easier success to the declared enemy. But Chānakya was not satisfied with the border areas. He had taken the vow to uproot the king, Purna vināsham vadāmi.

Chānakya had started placing and establishing his own men in Pātaliputra and the palace. He did not follow only the prescribed four ancient ways of Sāma, Dāma, Danda and Bheda but added three more of his own and followed them all as the preparation for the final blow. He treated all the persons who were insulted at the hands of the arrogant king or were angry with him as his friend and supporters. Whenever needed, he met them or sent messages. Inside the capital city and the palace he created and placed an assorted army for different purposes. He had bought together not only the army men and officials, ministers and influential Vaishyas but even prostitutes and their men.

He knew that most of the royal figures, ministers and officers were regular visitors of prostitutes. It was easier for him to mix intoxicants in the wine supplied to them. It did the trick. No one ever suspected

that the wine that they were taking had intoxicants. Secrecy was maintained painstakingly.

His numerous secret agents were doing their level best to take away one pillar after another to weaken the palace so that it could tumble down with one powerful thrust. It happened exactly in that way.

When all the necessary preparations were made, then one auspicious day, Chānakya came to Pātliputra with all the strength that he had mustered up. He placed them intelligently and covered all the key posts and points. His men were following the instructions to the letter.

Just after midnight, the whole of the small Mauryan army attacked the capital city and before the officials realized what was happening, they entered the palace. Most of the officials and higher authorities were captured and imprisoned from the kothās, residences cum work places of the prostitutes in an intoxicated state.

King Ghanānand was caught playing with selected young women. He was readily imprisoned in a half-naked state. Within hours and without bloodshed, all the royal persons and the king were imprisoned and the Nand dynasty was completely uprooted.

In the early hours of the morning of that colossal change, Chānakya took a bath, performed poojā and ceremoniously intertwined and bound his plait; the lock of hair at the crown of head that he had loosened in the court of the king Nand. It was done at the same spot where he had opened it while taking a vow. The last blow was successful and the vow was accomplished.

The Sun was brighter and happier that day.

Appraisal

One can't get that satisfaction which comes from small or big accomplishment as all our efforts are directed towards some accomplishment. That is final or ultimate which comes repeatedly in the life of a successful man and his life becomes a cluster of many finals won. Work with zeal and make concentrated effort to win all the finals that come your way.

Effect

The total gain is important. There is no doubt about it. But honest, concentrated effort is more valuable than all the gains which are the by-products of the effort.

Perfected Theory on Experiences

➤ The people of the town and cities would never survive without the works, production and system of the countryside. So, it is clear that the road to wealth, health and prosperity goes by the countryside.

➤ Only a balanced wage system can keep the balance in life, production and distribution while the modern system claims that the wages should not be fixed but negotiated and experts from the rival company or country should be bought at a higher salary. This way the loyalty also shifts which weakens the employees and they even lose faith. There are employees that get as low as two thousand per month and as high as two crores per month.

➤ Right kind of employees should be selected and given right training in such a way that they never feel bored with their nature of work. This way, they won't face stress, depression and strain. Among them, there should be right leaders or managers. The other employees will grow under a mentor.

➤ The employees must be motivated; they must know their powers and responsibilities. The powers and duties must be well-defined among the employees of different cadre taken for different purposes.

➤ Correct information must be easily passed in right urgency. The shirkers must be known and punished adequately: socially, psychologically and financially. Financial punishment is the weakest punishment. Before punishment, corrective measures should be taken. It will increase alertness.

➤ There must be a correct and effective strategy to face and defeat the opponents, competitors or kings.

➤ There must be a robust and correct internal accounting system so that no one can raise a finger against the payment or non-payment.

➤ Chānkaya or Kautilya or Vishnu Sharmā had very good advice for the entrepreneurs. They should never be in dilemma whether to venture it or not. They should be ethical and take needed training before venturing into a new project. After all, they are the bosses, they have to manage and control. Only that way, they can reach and stay at the top.

- Command but do not demand promotion in the job. Protect against all sorts of enemies: internal and external. Knowledge and training of a leader plays an important role. Correct, timely and profitable decision making, makes a leader.
- Pay your taxes in time to avoid complications.
- Don't opt for multiple projects. Get specialization. Never depend only on borrowed specialists.
- Kautilya lays stress on continuous learning of the king, the director or the chief executive and that of the workers.
- One can change job if one has acquired greater knowledge and skill but not for only money.
- If someone dies on duty then the employer should look after his family.
- Grab the right opportunity.
- Be an asset never a burden; be savior not a threat.
- Don't corrupt uncorrupt mind.
- The winner's sharpest weapon is secrecy.
- Don't worry about loss, multiply the gain.
- Be the strongest pillar but never a weak link.
- Manage the self to know how to manage others.

Chānakya had followed these methods and got success, so he mentioned all these things in his grand treatise. Of course, it had already taken a lot of time than what he desired but finally he succeeded in completely destroying Magadhnaresh and his Nand dynasty. It also took time since the aim was destruction of one and establishment of another powerful dyanasty.

4

Making of a King: the Chief

Chānakya was a learned man, a practical thinker, a proud Brāhmin, a conscious executive and an immaculate planner. He had taken the vow to completely destroy the Nand dynasty. His loosened the long and thick central lock behind his head that always reminded him that the vow is still to be fulfilled. He had the required plan to generate resources and raise an army to do the needful. He knew that he was not a warrior; that he was able to carry the books, not the sword; that he was a strategist, not a killer. He could lead an army from behind but he couldn't lead from the front. He needed a brave soldier, a lenient man, a disciplined disciple, a wise, strong and handsome youth, and a person who could mix with all without losing his individual status. He knew only such a person could fulfill his dreams, could execute his plans, change his ideas into reality and ascend the peak. He was looking for such a brilliant boy. Luck was on his side.

Search for the Future King

Chānakya established a hermitage where he started teaching the young students whom he wanted to train as soldiers and commanders. But whosoever was there with him, there was no one who showed the potential to be the king. So, Chānakya planned to move from village to village for material wealth to feed the students and to acquire weapons both for training and for the army to be raised; to recruit more and more young men to raise a big and expert army and to search for a "new king".

One day, in the plains of the Ganga, in a rich looking village full of greenery, he saw cows and cowboys. He was attracted to a tall boy who held his head high and was standing on a big stone. He was looking at the cattle and directing the boys. He was posing to be the king. Chānakya was engrossed in the drama. The boy sat on the stone as if it was the throne. He sent many boys as messengers and soldiers to do the tit-bits. When the boy saw Chānakya, he called him and when Chānakya approached him he asked:

"What do you want Learned Brāhmin?" The boy knew how to honour a Brāhmin.

Chānakya humbly replied, "I need cows to feed my pupils with milk."

The boy knew the value of charity. Without any hesitation he ordered, "This learned Brāhmin should be given one hundred and one cows."

Chānakya bowed humbly and asked, "Have you taken permission from your guardians?"

"A king does not need to take permission from others." The boy knew the powers of a king and was sure that he was doing something good. One must be charitable.

In the same mood Chānakya asked "Where are your parents?"

The boy directed his index finger towards the village. Chānakya

33

had already read the forehead and now he got the opportunity to read the palm. He saw what he wished to see. Now he was listening to the boy more intently.

The boy said, "I've no father. My mother lives there." The boy longed for the place.

"And what's the name of your mother." Chānakya wanted to know more.

"Mātā Murā" was the emotional reply.

"Victory to the king! I will come back to take the cows." Chānakya blessed the boy and turned towards the village.

He met the mother of the boy. The boy also joined them. He wanted to take the boy to make him a king. She was not willing to part with the only child she had. The boy was on the mother's side. Chānakya spent the whole evening and the whole night convincing them. The next morning was a bright morning. Chānakya took the boy and returned to his newly-established hermitage to educate and train him with the other young boys who were already taking training. In his eyes, they were the future soldiers, commanders, officials and ministers.

The boy was baptized. He was given a new name, Chandragupta, to which the name of his mother Mura was added as Maurya.

Appraisal

Painstaking and wise selection reduces the burden and tension. If manpower is not powerful and active then a lot is required to be done but with skillful and diligent manpower the expenses and time are drastically cut down.

Effect

Select the best and be relaxed; select the ordinary and remain always in doubt.

The training of the future king started. He planned everything meticulously for the boy from what to eat and what not; what to read and what not; from whom to meet and what to say to what not to say and whom to ignore. He prepared for him a routine and among the trainees he was declared the king so that he can imbibe the great qualities of a great and righteous future king.

Chānakya proved true to his words. He made him the king, Chandragupta Maurya, and started the Maurya dynasty, a great dynasty and that period is considered to be the golden period in ancient Indian history, but it took many years.

The village was Pippali Kānan, full of mango orchards in the Champakāranya. It was here that Rama stayed for two days while returning from Janakpur after the marriage with Sita. A pond was dug there which is known as "Sita Kunda". The mango grove is still there and there are two small temples: Shiva Temple and Rama Temple. It is some 120 kilometers from Patliputra in the north. After becoming the Minister and establishing the Maurya dynasty, Chānakya used to live here. He had special fascination for the place. Though his Fort, known as Chānaki Garha, is about 120 kilometers in the west from there in Narkatiaganj.

An Organization: An Empire

Relevance of the *Arthashāstra* in present times:

Chānakya knew that one or two things won't give him success and fulfill his dreams, so he was conscious of many things. Yet, he did not ignore his studies. He kept on reading the great treatises that he painstakingly collected. In the *Kautilya Arthashāstra*, at many places, Chānakya has mentioned many scholars who have given their ideas regarding the administration of an empire. Chānakya has opposed some views, explained many and accepted a few. It is enough to indicate that there were other works and treatises on the topic but there is none alive. It is the timelessness and agelessness of Chānakya's *Arthashāstra* that it is still alive and effective like its creator, the legendary and immortal figure who single-handedly changed the course of time and history of a nation divided in many small kingdoms.

People, even experts, usually think and say that whatever Chānakya has written in the *Arthashāstra* deals with the management of an empire and it is related to the powers and duties and training, etc., of an emperor. That is the difference between that time and modern time. Due to western influence all the kingdoms and empires have changed into Business Houses and Business Empires, the king and ministers and persons on different posts have changed into Managing Directors, Directors, and Executives on different scales and in different milieu. The portfolios have changed, the designations have changed but the responsibilities, duties, and powers have remained the same. There lies the similarity and if it is seen, read and understood in this light then the *Arthashāstra* is a superb book and has no peer.

If one asks: "Is this book, i.e the *Arthashāstra* written over thousands of years ago still applicable in today's world?"

The answer is ready for such a man: "Yes it is, because the *Arthashāstra* is a book about the management of the "living beings"; "life at large"; "human mind"; "human life"; "trade" and "natural resources", which has not changed a lot and the basics have remained the same since ages: both the resources and the work except heavy intrusion of machine which has created an army of unemployed persons in every country across the world. *So as long as the human mind remains filled with its negativities of jealousy, ego, hatred and over indulgence, so long as human beings require self control, discipline and management., 'Kautilaya's Arthashāstra will remain relevant.*

Chānakya in his world-famous book *Kautilya's Arthashāstra* has brought out some of the key business principles and strategies. Apart from the scholarly work, this book needs to be once again represented for practical application in today's world. The book has got many principles and techniques, and by applying thses we can bring tremendous improvements even in our day-to-day management.

An organization is definitely like an empire and the Managing Director or the Chief is the emperor that has an army of expert employees and workers and its complete marketing area its boundary or frontiers. The consumers of its products are the citizens that pay taxes in the form of profit. Many collaborators, dealers, sole distributors are friends and organizations in similar business are competitors, like enemies.

Everything that Kautilya has thought and said is for the safety, peace, prosperity and happiness of the state, such organizations, its directors and of its subject; both employees and users. His advice is not against any of the two: the ruler and the ruled; the master and the servant; or the employer and the employee.

Leadership Qualities

In an organization and in management, the leader rules and hence, leadership qualities are enhanced. Leadership is the ability to persuade others to seek predefined objectives enthusiastically is one part of the truth; the other part is that the leader must be wise enough to guide others whenever needed. There is no limitation of work and field. Those that lack leadership qualities are now starting virtual organizations and such virtual organizations are farce, and planned and created to mislead others. One must have that power as one has the authority and authority is the power and hence, needs power to utilize discretion in making decisions to be followed by others. Lack of wisdom and deviations create problems.

An organization is an institution for peace and prosperity. Its division in formal and Informal has nothing to do with its functioning. Both originate from work on similar patterns: deliberate or spontaneous. Its policies declare the ways the company is to deal with stakeholders, employees, customers, suppliers, distributors and other important and allied groups. In comparison to traditional business modern business organizations are unhealthy, feeble, vulnerable, instable and dependent while they vociferously claim the opposite.

Economic growth and the growth of business and business community can't be possible without the active cooperation and participation of non-business community.

It's in the long run and enlightened interest of corporations and commercial organizations to promote public welfare in a positive way, as they are capable of fighting and solving any social problem efficiently and effectively. A company growing and moving for diversification may need an entrepreneurial top management, while a large and well-established company may require more professionalism in management. The socio-cultural environment that consists of attitudes, beliefs, desires, expectations and customs of the society, determines the production, its distribution, price and even profit.

Effective and able managers must possess the following personal characteristics: decisive; aggressive; amiable; conforming; self-starting; productive; well informed; determined; energetic; creative; intelligent; responsible; enterprising; and clear thinking.

The principles of management are: to increase efficiency; to crystallize the nature of management; to carry on researches and to attain social objectives. There are some other very good principles for better management:

➤ Employ only the best, even on premium, at the key posts. It's the character, integration and sacrifice of the employees that make the difference. Depression in life and management is caused by lack of faith.

➤ Attend to your mails, get appreciated and accepted; throw your mails to dustbin, get rejected and thrown out from adorning eyes.

- It is easy to save own or others' money; it is difficult to save words and character. Those are happy that save.
- Complete each new work in a bit better way than the previous one. You will automatically grow better.
- Work for work, for pleasure, for honour, respect or all of them combined together but never work for money alone.
- Don't visit the places where you don't get respect, don't meet the persons who have no sense of propriety. Those persons are honourable that have life inside and God overhead.
- Don't allow doubt to creep into mind, keep faith and be faithful.
- If you want to win, win over your lust; if you want to grow, help others. The more you help the more help you get.
- Satisfaction is a boon and work is a blessing.
- Weigh the words that you say; not the money that you pay.
- If you live possessing or possessed by the universe your death is divine.
- Always do good you won't see bad days. Take a weapon swords will come out against you.
- Sleep after work; not during work.

An ideal king is one who has the highest qualities of leadership, intellect, energy and personal attributes.

The qualities of Leadership which attract followers and give success:

- Birth in a noble family
- Good fortune
- Intellect and prowess

- Association with elders
- Righteousness
- Truthfulness
- Resolute
- Enthusiastic
- Disciplined
- Honours promises
- Gratitude and gratefulness
- Lofty aims
- Not being dilatory
- Stronger than neighbouring kings/competitors and
- Possess ministers of high quality

The qualities in an Intellectual king

- Desire to learn
- Listening (to others)
- Grasping, retaining
- Understanding thoroughly and reflecting on knowledge
- Rejecting false views and adhering to the true ones

An energetic king is one who is

- Valorous
- Determined
- Quick, and
- Dexterous

An ideal king should be

- Eloquent
- Bold and endowed with sharp intellect

- Possess strong memory and a keen mind
- Amenable to guidance
- Well trained in all the arts and
- Be able to lead the army
- Be just in rewarding and punishing
- He should have the foresight to avail himself of the opportunities (by choosing) the right time, place and type of action.
- He should know how to govern in normal times and in times of crisis
- He should know when to fight and when to make peace, when to observe treaties and when to strike at an enemy's weakness.
- He should preserve his dignity at all times and not laugh in an undignified manner
- He should be sweet in speech, look straight at people and avoid frowning
- He should eschew passion, anger, greed, obstinacy, fickleness and backbiting
- He should conduct himself in accordance with the advice of elders

The Rājarishi: Guide Lines

The *Arthashāstra* deals in detail with the qualities and disciplines required for Rājarishi, a wise and virtuous king. With wise moves, patient teaching, continuous training and unmatched alertness Chānakya put all the great qualities in his new disciple and the future king Chandraguta Maurya. He has expressed those qualities in the *Arthashāstra*. One thing more, it is evident from his writings that he was not looking only for a simple replacement for the existing king but wanted to establish a righteous dynasty for a long time. So, he was not satisfied with the general qualities of a king but wanted to put in the higher and exceptional qualities too. He has declared:

"The king's happiness lies in the happiness of his subjects, their welfare is his welfare. He shall not consider as good only that which pleases him but treat as beneficial to him whatever pleases his subjects."

According to Kautilya, a Rājarshi is one who:

➤ Has self-control, having conquered the inimical temptations of the senses

➤ Cultivates the intellect by association with elders

➤ Keeps his eyes open through spies

➤ Is ever active in promoting the security & welfare of the people

➤ Ensures the observance by the people of their *dharma* by authority and example

➤ Improves his own discipline by continuous learning in all branches of knowledge

➤ Endears himself to his people by enriching them and doing good to them

Such a disciplined king should

➤ Keep away from another's wife;

➤ Not covet another's property;

➤ Practise *ahimsā*, non-violence towards all living beings

➤ Avoid day dreaming, capriciousness, falsehood and extravagance; and

➤ Avoid association with harmful persons and indulging in (harmful) activities.

Higher and Exceptional Qualities of a disciplined King

Abhigāmika Guna: Sublime family tradition; divine intelligence; embodiment of patience; farsightedness; Righteous; truthfully true; true to words and promises; gratefulness; highly ambitious; passionately enthusiastic; fast accomplishing ability; enchanting; determined and versed in scriptures.

Pragyā Guna: Knowledge of Scriptures; Discussions on Scriptures; minute receptivity; tenacious and retentive memory; specialization on known subjects; to draw deepest meaning through logical thinking and questioning; discard and disregard negativity; graciously accepting positive and rare qualities.

Utasāh Guna: Valour and bravery; intolerant and wrathful; nimbleness and oscillation; dexterity and efficiency.

Ātma Sampanna: Confident and resolute; mature and bold; impertinent and insolent; energetic and active; impudent and haughty; exceptional memory; excessive powerful; magnanimous; controlled and balanced; expert rider; saviour in calamity; benevolent; shy of asking; deep insight and far sight; wise and diligent in fight; enriching coffin without inflicting injury; pleasant; soft and sweet spoken; honour and respect for old and wise.

Qualities of **Township, Fort, Treasure, Army, Friends, Enemies**; have been discussed and given keeping very fine details in mind.

Duties of the King

If the king is energetic, his subjects will be equally energetic. If he is slack and lazy in performing his duties, the subjects will also be lax and thereby eat into his wealth. Besides, a lazy king easily falls into the hands of enemies. Hence, the Mahārāja should always be energetic. He shall divide the day and the night, each into eight periods of one and half hours, and perform his duties as follows:

Engagements in the Morning
- Receive reports on defence, revenue and expenditure
- Public audiences, to hear petitions of the city and country people

> Receive revenues and tributes; appoint ministers and other high officials and assign tasks to them

Engagements during Noon Hours

> Write letters and dispatches, confer with councillors
> Receive secret information from spies
> Personal: recreation, time for contemplation

Engagements during Evening Hours

> Personal: bath, meals, study
> Inspect review forces; Consult with the Chief of Defence

Engagements after Sunset

> Counseling with the secret agents
> Retire to the bed chamber to the sound of music, sleep

Engagements after Midnight

> Meditate on political matters and on work to be done
> Consult with councilors, send out spies

Engagements before Sunrise

> Religious, household and personal duties.

Meetings with his teacher, adviser on rituals, purohitas, personal physician, chief cooks and astrologer should be held regularly. A king or a chief can follow this or some other time table which suits him. Under his training, Chandragupta had to follow the routine irrespective of whether Chānakya was present in the hermitage or not. The result was that he started looking after and controlling the hermitage on the prescribed pattern without minute to minute interference and advice of his learned teacher.

The king/director or the chief shall be ever active in the management of the economy. The root of wealth is activity and lack of it brings material distress. In the absence of fruitful economic activity, both current prosperity and future growth will be destroyed. A king can achieve the desired objectives and abundance of riches by undertaking (productive) economic activity.

Birth of a Prince: An Heir

With Chandragupta in the forefront, Chānakya demolished the Nand dynasty and established the Maurya dynasty. Many smaller kingdoms and the living relatives and friends of King Ghanānad could not digest this; rather they hated both Chānakya and Chandragupta. They were always busy in conspiring to kill them. Chandragupta was under constant threat and vulnerable too. He did not realize the danger but Chānakya knew it and was conscious about the safety of the emperor. Only he knew what had he done to select, prepare and train a righteous and powerful king for the country.

He was unable to control the thoughts of the friends of Nand or the lust of his relatives. They were getting a lot of money and an opportunity to lead a luxurious life without doing much. The new king declared end of luxury to them. So, they were attempting to kill the emperor.

Once, a guptachar (spy) of another kingdom, disguised as an envoy, came to meet Chandragupta. Chānakya was suspicious. His secret agents gave him the feedback and true identity of the spy and his intention to kill the emperor. *The meeting was arranged. The envoy went inside to meet him but an alert Chānakya kept an eye on them from behind the curtain with his own men ready for action.*

Though the two were alone but three others were watching them. The envoy talked of the sweet sorbet of his country and offered a bottle. He prepared two glasses of sorbet and handed over one to Chandragupta. When the king was about to drink it, Chānakya dramatically came out from behind the curtain, stopped Chandragupta from taking the drink and ordered the arrest and death of the secret agent.

Chandragupta was stunned while Chānakya showed impeccable outer patience while he was boiling with anger from inside. His anxiety about the king and restless for his safety grew.

This was one stray incident but five more followed in a short span of time. Chānakya knew that the there is no end to the conspiracy towards a ruler. Then the only remedy is the strength of the ruler. He was assured of Chandragupta's physical strength, war acumen, and winning ability. None could defeat him but he was worried about the deceptive moves. Chandragupta seldom had doubt about the integrity of others.

Worried and able Chānakya decided to make the emperor's systems immune towards poison. He started administering a little poison in every meal to Chandragupta. It was done secretly by the chief royal cook. It went on for years. As Chānakya was an expert of medicines and poisons so he knew the fatal doze and healthy doze. He would himself prepare different kinds of poisons for the king.

Three queens were married to Chandragupta in separate ceremonies. They were Helen, Durdha and Chitrā. The second Queen Durdha was in the ninth month of pregnancy when a deadly incident occurred. The queen was weak and carrying a child. Chandragupta tried to give more time to her. They were expecting the son, the prince and heir of the Maurya Empire. He cared a lot about the queen.

The usual meal was served to the king with a bit of poison. Out of love and care, the king invited the queen to share the meal. The cook lost his *wit. In place of stopping them on this or that ground or pretext, he ran up to Chānakya to inform. Chānakya rushed towards them.*

In the meantime, the queen had taken a few morsels of the king's food. Her tender body and system could not digest it. It was late when Chānakya reached there. The queen was losing her consciousness. He wanted the heir and was worried about the poison passing on to the foetus. It would ruin everything.

Chānakya could not wait for the Vaidyas to administer medicines. Seconds were precious. Time was passing swiftly. At that moment, conscious Chānakya opted for surgery. In that very room, he operated upon the queen and took out the child from her womb. He saved the heir but could not save the queen who died because of the poison and the profuse blood that oozed out during the operation.

Chānakya may have read and known about surgery but it needs a lot of practise to operate on a person. He lacked that practise. It was his steady mind and grand memory that saved the heir but it was the mistake that took the life of the queen.

The foetus had taken a bindu (drop) of visha, (poison), the negative essence of plants, so he was named Bindusār. Chānakya fostered and trained the Prince. Bindusār was made the crown prince first, then the king of the great Maurya Empire in the lifetime of both Chandragupta and Chānakya. He too revered Chānakya and followed his advice to rule well over Greater India.

Appraisal

Patience is the hidden but constantly working power of a person. Only with patience one can keep a watch; learn and analyze the inside information and take timely, needed and correct action to get the desired result. The greater the patience, the greater is the success.

Training of a Future King

Chānakya knew and believed in the importance of self-discipline. Discipline is of two kinds – inborn and acquired. There must be an innate capacity for self-discipline for the reasons given below. Instruction and training can promote discipline only in a person capable of benefiting from them; people incapable of natural self-discipline are not benefited. Learning imparts discipline only to those who have the following mental facilities:

➤ Obedience to a teacher
➤ Desire and ability to learn
➤ Capacity to retain what is learnt
➤ Understanding what is learnt
➤ Reflecting on acquired knowledge
➤ Ability to make inferences by deliberating on facts

Those who are devoid of such mental faculties are not benefited by any amount of training. One who will be a king should acquire discipline and follow it strictly in life by learning the sciences from authoritative teachers.

The Training of a Prince

With improving self-discipline, the prince should always associate with learned elders, for in them alone has discipline its firm roots. For a trained intellect ensues yoga, successful application, from yoga comes self-possession. This is what is meant by efficiency in acquiring knowledge. Only that king will enjoy the earth unopposed who is wise, disciplined, devoted to a just governance of the subjects and conscious of the welfare of all beings.

Before the change and establishment of the Maurya dynasty, Chānakya trained Chandragupta and after the establishment he trained Prince Bindusār also. He did not live a relaxed life. For one who wishes to create and govern a large and great organization there is no free and relaxed moment. His pupils knew it, and followed the dictates of their teacher sincerely.

6

Enemy of an Enemy is a Friend

Magadha King Ghanānad was not a wise and strong ruler. He was arrogant and lascivious. Both his people and employees were against him but because of his known cruelty no one had the guts to speak openly against him. In his arrogance, the king forgot his duties and responsibilities and even the fact that people make a kingdom and people can give a throne or dethrone a king. Chānakya must have known it. He must have seen with his own eyes on his long way from south to the northeast of the vast country. When they learnt of the enmity of Chānakya, his open declaration of the ruin of the Nand dynasty, and about his hot preparations against him, they stood behind him without coming into the open. Chānakya declared it very late in his book but the people followed the concept that the *enemy of an enemy is a friend*.

It was just a chance that one day, Vaishyas, Pandas and rich farmers from the Gayā Region, a pilgrim centre; Mithilā Region and Vaishāli region came separately to meet him. Chānakya had some prior information because his espionage system, though small yet was on the track and working smoothly. Wherever he had gone, he had made friends and without appointing them as Guptachar, had given them the responsibility of Guptachars in his own effective way. Since, he had inkling into what was happening and who were eager to meet him so, he created the circumstance that they reached there on the same day. Perhaps, he wanted to prove to them that he

had the unconditional support of many from different regions. He did it cleverly.

Chānakya preferred to talk to the men from the Gayā Anchal as it was closer to Patliputra and had greater influence on the state of affairs. People from Vaishāli were closer and Mithila too were not far away but they had, in fact, no say in the political upheavals. They were peaceful and liked to live their life in their own way, which was of late disturbed.

He went up to the door of the largest hut in the hermitage to welcome the visitors. The leader introduced himself as Abhoy Shroff, a traditional goldsmith by profession. The others were not named though Chānakya knew the contingent but he did not mention it.

They placed their problems and concluded:

"We are ready to sacrifice for the health, prosperity and peace in the region. We are suffering in stead of living."

"It is too early to enter into a treaty but it's the word of a teacher that you will get the best deal when Chandra Maurya comes to throne. Both agriculture and business will be taken care of. The forests will yield and the rivers will irrigate more. People will be safe and satisfied," Chānakya clarified and gave confidence.

"In expectation of that return, we will manufacture and supply weapons along with expert and young men and regular and adequate material," they assured.

"Governance is all about security, safety and growth, which will be ensured. It is not an assurance, it is a fact. From tomorrow onwards, the *Māgadhi Soldiers or officers will not come to you."* Chānakya declared.

"How can it be possible?" They expressed their doubt.

"Four main officers in your area were killed last night. Both the ways leading to your area are under surveillance and protected, rather sealed. No army will be allowed to pass through those main routes. Your men are making preparation to take their charge today." Chānakya opened some secrets that his fistful daring soldiers had performed to take the full and unconditional support of the people.

"You are working fast. It's an excellent job." They praised with great relief as they usually prayed to be free from the four notorious persons of the area who were very close to the king and controlled everything. They checked their pleasure which was fast turning into ecstasy, ready to hear more.

"Not only I but all are busy performing their duties. A country is not safe if its people are not safe."Chānakya showed his confidence.

"We have some loaded carts with us. Please accept and treat it as the first of its kind." They stood up to take leave.

Later on, Chānakya met the other groups and the talk was almost similar with similar result. This sort of attitude of the people never allowed Chānakya to feel shortage of man, money and material as he managed the three meticulously well. It proved to be the basis of his tremendous success.

Fortunately for him, the time was ripe for revolt and the anger of the mass had started overflowing. Simply because of their support, his and the movements of the Maurya Army was not reported in time for officials to react and act.

Chānakya knew that people had the power and both Nand's people and personnel were against him ready to shift their loyalty. He has discussed these aspects in his book in detail. Moreover, he knew the value of small places, scattered hands and its honest and diligent people.

The Power of People or Employees

Although, Chānakya kept everyone under surveillance but he had empowered the employees of the Maurya dynasty. Of course, they were not allowed to act arbitrarily or do wrong but they possessed immense power, and had the authority to question anyone.

In modern context "employee empowerment" is not only a management buzzword but the employees and employers are coming closer and working hand in glove as they know that their survival depends on the success of the organization, and the success of an organization depends on the combined power and effort of the employees and the employers.

The employees are being given greater power and full accountability for the results, as they own the total responsibility of the work. That way the employees are being motivated and actually, they feel motivated and try their best to fulfill the responsibility. Their latent abilities are also utilized in a positive and constructive way. That is a sort of initiative and encourages an employee to perform his/her very best. Naturally, the employees should be given the liberty to perform their role to perfection to the extent their personal ability permits. This gives a lot of advantage to the organization. The organizers are sure and confident of the accomplishments of the given targets because they know that their employees are giving their best.

Employee empowerment adds to their positive thinking, approach and productivity. They feel that they are recognized and appreciated. The organization that does not give power to its employees suffers on many counts. They invariably run a race against time, because either they unnecessarily waste time talking to the immediate Boss for instruction or rushing to the head. It slows down the productivity. The employees lack self motivation and personal participation.

Modern executives too agree now that by giving employees paradigm to take decisions pertaining to their team, the customers and the work environment are bound to help them execute their role better and for greater advantage of the organization. The employees get a freehand to operate and take independent decision in the best interest of the organization and its employees. Naturally; they are all the time on their toes looking for something that needs immediate attention.

This gives an employee a sense of ownership, clarity in objectives and role that makes him/her more focused and goal-oriented. They prepare themselves for the next customer, next day, next month and thus for future. It gives job satisfaction and builds confidence. Such free yet dedicated employees, like Chānakya and his employees will always be assets. Anyway, one must feel responsible for the results, for own actions and the actions of the subordinates and show one's best "always".

Shifting Loyalty: Changing Organization

It is not that Chānakya had no idea and information about changing an organization for better and higher opportunity or when one disliked the chief, or when the chief was angry or when there were some disputes. In 4:93:5, entitled "Samaya Āchārikam" behaviour according to time and need Chānakya has given more than half a dozen examples when on trivial-looking incident the ministers left their kings:

➤ *Ayam uchaih: sinchititi Kātyāyanah pravavrāja.* The King said, "The labourer is irrigating from above." His Minister Kātyāyana left him.

➤ *Kraucha upasavyam iti Karniko Bhārdwājah.* The Krauch has flown from the left side. Heard Karnika from Bhārdwāja Gotra and left his king.

➤ *Trinam iti Deeraghah Chārāyana.* Āchārya Deergha Chārāyana left his king after looking at a straw.

➤ *Sheetā shātiti ghotamukhah.* Āchārya Ghota Mukha left his king when he heard him saying, "The clothe is cold".

➤ *Hasti pratyaukshiditi Kinjalkah.* The Minister named Kinjalka left his king when he saw him pouring water on the back of an elephant.

➤ *Rathāshwa prāshansiditi Pishunah.* Āchrya Pishuna left his king when he heard him praising the horse of the chariot.

➤ *Prati ravane shunah pishunputrah iti.* The son of that Pishuna left his king when he saw a dog barking at him.

Despite the above eye opening examples, Chānakya was always against shifting loyalty. The monetary gain may be far more than the expectations yet Chānakya won't allow or advise anyone to hop up or switch over to another organization. The person hopping now and then, and shifting loyalty from one company to another loses creditability. Chānakya could have accepted anything but not any weakness in character and determination. Once one accepted the job, he took some responsibility and some wages. He knew the conditions. In the meantime some changes took place, in all probability that "one" person got experience and grew from inside. Now he is more skilled, better equipped and possesses greater ability. It may be worth more than what salary he is getting from the place. So, he tries and gets a better placement or some other company shows interest and tries to buy the man on higher salary. If the person denies the offer and remains with the parent organization, he shows character and confidence and is later on rewarded by holding a key and more responsible post but if he switches over to another company, he would get the agreed salary but he could never win the confidence in the 2nd company, and will never be given any key post. Chānakya had that in mind when he said:

Tatra astho dosha nirghātam mitraih bhartari cha ācharet;
Tato bhartari jived wā mrite wā punah ābrajet.

(If there is some dispute or complain or anger, an employee should remain in the service of the master and clarify the situation through his friends or dear ones, and please him. One can leave that service when the original master dies.)

Nowadays, several employees, in quest to boost up their career prospects, resort to job hunting and hopping often without thinking about its pros and cons. They think, at present professional growth is only possible if one looks out for better options, and periodically change the organization that one works for.

That is also a reason that the companies are bent upon paying a meager starting salary as they know that the person would switch to some other company the moment he learns the tricks of the trade and gets adequate experience. They don't believe in them.

Some modern experts are also thinking in the line of Chānakya, "Changing job frequently reflects badly on one's resilience and loyalty to one's firm. If one is not loyal to one how can he/ she be expected to be loyal to others."

The following negative qualities come out to the fore: lower motivational level, and restlessness and lack of direction, and immature approach to a workplace.

In the interviews their commitment and loyalty to their previous employer are questioned. One question is very common, "Why do you want to leave them?"

It is double-edged hidden knife. If you show your own weakness your chances of getting the job become dim, and if you blame the parent company and if they happen to know the organizers of the company then you are labeled as a liar. You neither possess a definite philosophy nor have clear vision of your career goal.

Other questions follow closely. Some about the past experience and talent; the required job skills; fit to the concerned job profile and eye-brows are raised on the character, integrity, sense of responsibility and ability to do justice to the new post and organization. Believe it or not but a job-hopper's resume is always scrutinized minutely by recruiters and perspective employers. Yet Chānakya has shown advantages of changing organization which is given elsewhere, employees, ``Employees Behaviour towards Employer'' (P.157).

The Edge of Smaller Places

Chānakya led others through examples. He lived in a very simple way and had great and the most practical thoughts. He preferred smaller places. The smaller places have a clear edge over the metros.

In India smaller markets are cash markets; and smaller places have latent talent. For talent search and for consumption of the produce smaller places are really very suitable. It was the place from where Chānakya got Chandragupta who became a Chakravarti Samrāt; and from such places he collected an army of dedicated persons. Gandhiji laid a lot of stress on it as well as cottage industry in order to foster the people and their talent. Of late, the big organizations have realized this small fact of the potentialities of smaller places; and as a result they have created smallest possible packs of their products that have sold like hot cakes. Naturally, they are sending their marketing officers and appointing area managers. They have appointed representatives cum sale promoters in all the districts.

Low Cost and Low Risk Entrepreneurship

There were very few people who knew India – from its different social, various climates to different food and living habit. In the ancient period Chānakya was one person and in the modern period Gandhi was another known person who knew India well. Others usually look at a part and declare it to be the whole. The tropical climate from 8 degree North to 37 degree North saves it from both too hot and too cold. In between, India lies and enjoys the changes that occur from very hot in Kerala to very cold in Kashmir. This gives India a balanced climate; naturally Indians are balanced people, balanced thinkers and balanced workers: with knowledge and skill of different types. So, it has a great skilled work force. It reduces the cost. The density of population ensures sale. As a result, the entrepreneurship in India is easier with low cost and low risk. Apprenticeship here costs virtually nothing.

The rural population in India still accounts for 70%. If suburban population is added to it, it will be well over 80%. It represents "big growth opportunity" that must be tapped into and clearly some organizations are taking earnest steps towards it.

One thing more, over 55% of Indian people are below the age of 25 years and needs the infrastructure and opportunity to up skill and educate themselves in order to deeply and effectively participate in the overall development of the country, particularly in the natural living condition and economic development. India has the opportunity to grow bigger, greater and stronger.

What distinguished India from Western infrastructure system is the climate and milieu of the country. We are not in a cold region. Unlike the west we are in tropical zone where we neither get extreme heat nor extreme cold. Hence, closed rooms are least needed here while it is imperative in west otherwise they won't cope with the extreme cold and snow fall.

On the contrary, we need a lot of air and open space. The infrastructure is taking its toll both on the mental and physical health of the employees as well as the lion's share from the capital. In every field of industrial entrepreneurship and also in government sector many big industries at thousands of places proved white elephant and burdened the governments with huge loans because the production is less than 20% of the planned and established capacity. No other example will be needed if one turns one's head towards power sector. Not a single unit is producing electricity to its capacity. Many units are sick or dead. It's true from Pataratu to Kanti. It is because of the high investment in infrastructure. All the structures were constructed first including the quarters for employees but there is insignificant production. They incur heavy loss every year which is eventually growing as loan on the heads of the people. It is that sort of bad investment that the free Indians in 1950 are each under the loan of about eight thousand which they don't know.

Low cost entrepreneurship is always a success. There is a tale almost everywhere that each industrial house has grown up from the least investment at the initial stage, only some two generations back.

That is the greatest reason that low cost and low risk entrepreneurship is always successfull while high cost and high risk factories have badly failed. As a result about 85% of the industries started in India are either sick or dead.

The CEOs must think and plan educating people and giving intensive and extensive training for overall gain of the organizations. The initial investment will be easily paid back in multiple ways. It is heartening that many business houses have entered the field of education and training but sadly enough they are attracting the rural population to come to grown and developed urban areas. They are not reaching the people, which would be the best way to tap the talent and energy. If one is looking for raw and right talent, the rural areas are the best place to look for. The organizations in this field are very few and clustered at certain places. There is immense scope in this field. An organization can succeed even if all the facilities are not available there; and even if they are unable to provide all the facilities. The talents are such that can be groomed with "a little".

7

Creation from Debris

"Move forward in groups as a part of the mass, not together marching as army. Don't fight as if in battle ground. Attack when the enemy is unprepared from five sides with one group in reserve to in-enforce the weakening one."

"At whatever place you are always be in possession of your sense faculty attentive and alert. Listen to all sounds and mark each movement around with undivided attention with open eyes, clear years and perceptive mind. React fast without showing reaction or surprise. Catch opponents by surprise without giving the time to react."

"Be in close vicinity but away from the central places looking at it with vigilant mind. Mark the movements and read the faces of each one coming out or going in. Divert the subtle energy of hurt ego to the hands while hitting, to the legs while escaping but always to the mind."

"Destroy the King but save the people. Demolish the palace but stamp not the crops. Ransack the pubs but not the markets."

Chānakya had given definite and standing orders to his enthusiastic soldiers and re-enforcement civil battalion. It worked and was effective. He had learnt his practical lessons from the initial setbacks that he got from the alert officials and soldiers *when he tried to attack on the centre with a view to win the palace itself but the palace was well guarded.*

After realizing the difficulties and foolishness of the attacks in the beginning, moving in the lines standing at ease after rigorous training Chānakya usually gave the instruction and announced strategy.

Appraisal

Only an alert mind keeps the sense organs alert. The priority must be clear in one's mind as well as what is to b e done and what is not. Alertness will always give a way out from deep, dense, dark woods of worldly affairs.

Effect

One must save the life in all circumstances as the continuity of life is essential for survival of human beings.

In strange style and short time, Chānakya wiped out the Nand dynasty. In the same ways and in an amazing fashion he brought a big and varied country like India under one rule. He applied all the methods that he has dictated in his immortal books: luring some, creating fear in some, entering into treaty with many, fighting battles and defeating the rigid ones but he brought them together and united the whole country that included many foreign lands of the modern world. During his time they were integral parts of Brihattar Bhārat, Greater India.

After winning the Magadha kingdom, he opened his plans one by one to make a strong empire. It is the way to establish an empire or an organization. He followed this path and made the Maurya Empire a great, united and lasting dynasty.

The whole existence depends on work and earning. The sun works and gets feedback of energy as fuel; the planets move and get energy from sun and other planets and stars; the earth moves and works and stores energy in return for changing garbage into minerals, vitamins and jewels and so it sustains. It is true to all living being but there is greater responsibility on man besides work, earning, storing and saving everything because he has consciousness and conscience both. He knows, he can think, co-relate and save or destroy. But his existence depends on working and earning.

In modern context and language, this working and earning comes under Human Resources and Finance. He possesses immense wealth inside. Nature provides a lot for growing more and consuming in moderate fashion. Man or none is allowed to waste anything. Wastage is ruin whether it is of wealth or health or relation or character or morality or humanity.

Organizations are also like that only. Kingdoms are also no exceptions. Orgamizations work and get the wages. If it is a business organization then either it produces something or provides some sort of service. In both the cases, either they get profit or service charges but **every business is reciprocal, and depends on mutual give and take**.

Chānakya knew it well and hence, he laid a lot of stress on ethical deeds, concentrated effort, hard labour and material. In his opinion man and material was important, money was not because money was a by-product of ability, skill, diligence and material. Mines and minerals are important; land and buildings are important. **Ironically enough, the value of land and material and ability always grows but the buying capacity of money always comes down.**

During the last forty years the value of gold has increased hundred times and that of land one thousand times and of labour in the form of salary, has ioncreased 200 times and the value of money has reduced in that very proportion. Why so? Because **money is not a thing, it has no value of its own. It is only a means of exchange.** The value of a material, a product, labour or service is fixed in money and paid in money. Money has that much significance.

That is the reason that Chānakya in his *Kautilya Arthashāstra* declared that all business and industry dealing with minerals should be controlled by the governing body. Its Capital, Labour, Management and Income must be in the hands of the king, the supreme power of the kingdom. He has mentioned: *Sonā; Chāndi; Tāmbā; Sheeshā; Tin; Lohā; Mani; Lavana,* etc.

Kautilya gave other business and industries to public sector as private property to be controlled and managed by individuals or groups. They had complete rights on them. Among them, he has mentioned: *kheti; soota; shilp; go-pālan; ashwa pālan; hasti- pālan; Surā; mānsa; veshyālaya; manoranjan; nritya-sangeet; gāyan-vādan,* etc.

But Kautilya insists that each business and transaction, related to production, distribution and consumption, must be wisely controlled by the government or the body designated for the work with different duties and responsibilities. The control and ownership of all activities is under the governance to enrich the treasure and to avoid deception by the common man or even officials.

For an organization rich treasure is essential. So, Kautilya has given preference to treasure, its safety, the ways to enrich it, the resources of income, the heads of expenditure and also excess and waste expense. He has thought over them in very subtle way and divided them in different catagories for smoorh handling and running.

Kautilya has fixed duties, responsibilities and powers of each one in the administration of Finance. It is true to *Samāhartā*: Chief of all Finance and Storage. He collected all sorts of taxes and entered into his "Sealed Register". He had *Sannidhātā*: Chief of Treasure to assist and many other officials to work under him. The others are:

➤ *Sthānika*: He controlled ¼ of the Janapada.

➤ *Gope*: The authority that controlled the villages.

- *Pradeshthā*: Assistant to Sthānika and Gope.
- *Aksha Patal Adhyaksha*: Accountant General.
- *Koshādhyaksha/ Artha Kārnika*: Chief Accountant.
- *Kārmika*: Assistant to Chef Accountant.
- *Gananikya*: Record Keeper of villages.
- *Sānkhyānaka*: Census Officer; Statistical Officer.
- *Lekhak*: Clerk.
- *Nivi Grāhak*: Assistant.
- *Gopālaka*: Assistant.
- *Apayukta*: Assistant.
- *Nidhānaka*: Assistant.
- *Prati Grāhak*: Assistant.
- *Nibandhak*: Registrar.
- *Dāyak*: Assistant.
- *Maitri Vaiyāvrityak*: Assistant.

Kautilya has divided their works in six divisions called:
- *Karaniya*
- *Siddha*
- *Shesha*
- *Āya*
- *Vyaya*
- *Nivi*

He further divides Karaniya into six other divisions:
- *Sansthān*
- *Prachār*
- *Sharira Avasthān*
- *Ādān*

- *Sarva Samudaya Pinda*
- *Sanjāt*

Siddha too has been divided in six sub categories:

- *Koshārpita*
- *Rājahār*
- *Purvya*
- *Par Samvatsar Anuvriita*
- *Shāshan Mukta*
- *Mukhāgyapta*

Shesha too has six categories:

- *Siddha Prakarna Yoga*
- *Danda Shesha*
- *Balātkrit Pratistabdha*
- *Avashrista*
- *Asār*
- *Alpasār*

Āya, Income has been divided in three main categories and one sub-category:

- *Vartamān*: Daily Income
- *Paryushita*: It includes Balance of Previous Years and Income from enemy countries
- *Anyajāt*: It includes lost or forgotten property or income; income from crimes and criminals; other than taxes; gifts; looted from enemy army; the wealth that has no claimant;
- *Vyaya Pratyāya*: the remaining amount from army expenses, construction expenses, income from price rise, excess income from business competitors, fines from wrong weighing and measurement.

Vyaya, Expenditure has also been divided in four categories:

➤ *Nitya*: Daily Expense;

➤ *Nitya Utapādika*: Excess Expense in Daily Expenditure

➤ *Lābha*: The money spent for fortnightly, monthly and annual income;

➤ *Lābha Utpādika*: Excess expense on the *Lābha* category.

Nivi is the balance after calculating all the income and expenditures. It is divided in two categories:

➤ *Prāpta*: Already deposited in the Treasure;

➤ *Anuvritta*: Expected to be deposited in the treasure soon.

Embezzlement and Misappropriation of Money

Kautilya had thought deeply about embezzlement and misappropriation of collected money by the chiefs and other officials. He must have collected the information in detail through his *Guptachars* regarding the ways the embezzlement was appropriated by different personnel in different area and departments. He has instructed the king or the modern directors:

➤ To control the money to enrich the treasure;

➤ To keep vigil on the character of the heads;

➤ To stop theft of all types;

➤ To encourage all related production;

➤ To encourage the sale of the produce of land and water;

➤ To save life and stock from flood and fire;

➤ To ensure timely payments in different heads;

➤ To see that all collections are deposited in the treasure; in modern context, in the bank and definitely in the correct account.

In 2:14:28 entitled "*Samudasya Yukta Apahritsya Pratya-ānayanam*, Kautiulya has listed eight types of embezzlements and misappropriation of treasure: *pratibandhah prayogo vyavahār avastārah parihāpan upabhogah parivartanam upahārah cha iti kosha kshayah*; and also the punishment for each type of embezzlement:

➤ **Pratibandha**: The three types of *pratibandha* are:

a. to fail to collect money, mostly taxes;

b. to fail to keep in own hand the collected money and

c. to fail to deposit it at proper and designated place. Such an official will have to pay back ten times the embezzled money.

➤ **Prayoga**: By trying to multiply the collected money by investing or by giving as loan on interest is called *prayoga*. Such officials should be fined double the embezzled amount.

➤ **Vyavahār**: To indulge in business with the money taken from treasure is called *vyavahār*. The punishment is to give double the amount.

➤ **Avastār**: The official who deliberately delays the collection of money to harass the people and to take more than the due, is called *avastār*. Such official should pay five times the original sum.

➤ **Parihāpan**: Because of inability or mismanagement the official who fails to collect money and increases the expenses is called *parihāpan*. He should be fined four times the original sum.

➤ **Upabhoga**: To use corporate or government money for self or relatives is called *upabhoga*. If he uses jewels then he should be hanged; if he uses general articles then the articles should be seized and its price will be the punishment.

➤ **Parivartan**: To replace costly articles or materials with others is called *parivartan*. The punishment should be equal to loss.

➤ **Apahār:** There are three types of *apahār*:

a. collected money is not entered into the register;

b. showing expense without spending, and

c. to deny to have collected the money. Such officials should be forced to pay twelve times more than the original money.

In the same chapter Kautilya has discussed in detail that the Chief can embezzle or misappropriate money in forty ways.

Resolving Quarrel

Kautilya says: "Quarrels among people can be resolved by winning over the leaders or by removing the cause of the quarrel. People fighting among themselves help the king by their mutual rivalry. Conflicts for power within the royal family, on the other hand, bring about harassment and destruction to the people and double the exertion that is required to end such conflicts. Hence internal strife in the royal family for power is more damaging than quarrels among their subjects. The king must be well versed in knowing others, discerning ability and shrewd in judgement."

Virtues and Vices

Vices are corruptions due to ignorance and indiscipline; an unlearned man does not perceive the injurious consequences of his vices. He summarizes: subject to the qualification that gambling is most dangerous in cases where power is shared. The vice with the most serious consequence is addiction to wine and other such drinks, followed by, lust for women, gambling, and hunting.

8

Dealing with Problems

Once, Chānakya met an officer of the palace, Mātanga, on a bridge. Although it appeared to be a casual meeting but it was actually arranged. It was almost noon and there was virtually no movement on the bridge. He was neglected and repeatedly ignored by the king. Chānakya was eager to tap all such resources from where he could learn secrets and gain support at the time of actual overthrow. He was determined to split the opposition, to create suspicion and division to weaken the whole set up.

After casual talk and exchange of formal salutations Chānakya said: "Your Matta and Angas are precious to be weighed in jewels."

"Jewels I have accumulated but honour I have none," Mātanga admitted.

"Honour is the best jewel in the garland of a man. My hands are eager to put the garland with that brightest jewel around the neck of the most deserving person." Chānakya was opening up.

"The lowly figure with energy in dust can't be a deserving person." He was too broken to show his ego.

"Revolutionists anoint their foreheads with dust from the Mother Land. Eternal Mother likes it." He was weighing the patriotic impulse.

"Mother will get the head whenever needed." He promised.

"The Mother will safely and lovingly keep that son in her lap." It was a counter promise.

"I will salute the Sunrise." It was another firm promise.

"Such sons never get swayed by Sunsets." The hint was clear. They parted after formal salutations.

Appraisal

Success depends on the spirit behind the work. The effort is far greater and superior in the highly spirited, patriotic and spiritual person than in the lowly persons with only physical pleasure as the aim of life. The hunger will not generate as much energy as the safety in a do or die situation.

Effect

One should not leave a single stone unturned while striving for success because failure shows lack of effort.

Split and Weaken

Kautilya recommended seven strategies in dealing with the neighbouring powers to the highest official, the king and through him to all foreign affairs ministries and others who regularly dealt with unknown and strange people. With the following mantra people of any place can be controlled. One must remember that all of them are not used at one time. If one fails the other can be applied or if one is used towards one set of people then another can be used towards another set. It all depends on the need, urgency and the kind of people one is dealing with. The strategies are:

➤ **Sāma**: Appeasement, non-aggression pact
➤ **Danda**: Strength, punishment
➤ **Dāna**: Gift, bribery

- **Bheda**: Divide, split, separating opposition
- **Māyā**: Illusion, deceit
- **Upekshā**: Ignoring the enemy
- **Indrajāla**: Showing army and spiritual strength

Kautilya's opinion

"For the guard not reporting to the city-superintendent an offence committed during the night whether by the animate or the inanimate, the punishment shall be in conformity with the offence, also in case of negligence."

"The king or the CEO should strive to give training to the prince."

Leaders at the top should completely focus on developing the potential leaders. Who is a leader and how to identify him is a challenge in itself. One will realize that a person successful in one area can be a failure in another area. Or one who is a successful leader in a particular group may be a failure while leading another.

The leader should be serious towards security lapses. This means, how an alert security person should be. He has to report every single offence committed to his superiors. He cannot take any seen or unseen movements for granted. If the security official does not do that even the security personnel shall be punished. A special focus has to be given to corporate security personnels.

Wildlife and Forests

The Mauryas first looked at the forests as a resource. For them, the most important forest product was the elephant. Military might in those times depended not only on horses and men but also on battle-elephants. It resulted in the defeat of Seleucus, Alaxender's governor of Panjab. The Mauryas sought to preserve supplies of elephants since it was more cost- and time-effective to catch, tame and train wild elephants than raise them. The *Arthashāstra* devotes a few chapters to it and unambiguously specifies the responsibilities of officials such as the *Protector of the Elephant Forests.*

On the border of the forest, the king should establish a forest for elephants guarded by foresters. The superintendent will, with the help of the guards, protect the elephants whether along the mountain, along a river, along lakes, or in marshy tracts. They should kill anyone slaying an elephant.

The *Arthashāstra* also reveals that the Mauryas designated specific forests to protect supplies of timber, as well as lions and tigers, for skins. Elsewhere the *Protector of Animals* also worked to eliminate thieves, tigers, and other predators to render the woods safe for grazing cattle.

Present rulers and administrators lack those qualities laid down by Kautilya. It is highly desirable and needed that they are endowed with similar qualities and rise up to similar height. In countries where the forests are, the progress has been meteoric, both macro and micro.

In the 2nd *Adhikaran*, 24th *Prakaran* and 8th *Adhyāya*, Kautilya enlists 40 ways of scams. If the scam is not proved then the complainant should be punished, but if the complaint is proved, then both physical and financial punishments must be given to the related person. No one should be forgiven or allowed to move scot free: *Anishpanne shāriram haiyah anyam wā dandam labhet; na cha anugrāhya.* If the scam is proved 1/6th of the amount, *shatam ansham labhet,* should be given to the informer but if the informer or the complainant accepts bribe and turns in favour of the culprit then he should be sentenced to death:

> *Nishpatau nikshipedvadam ātmānam wāpawahyayet;*
> *Abhiyukta upajāpātu suchako badham āpanuyāt.*

Documentation Skill: Shāsanādhikār

In the 2nd Adhikaran, 2:26:10 Kautilya has talked not only about keeping an eye on the officials and knowing about their moral and immoral character, sincerity or dishonesty, but he has gone to the extent to declare that everything should be in black and white. There must be written treaties and written orders. Not only this, he has discussed types of documents, how to prepare the documents and what type of errors can one commit while preparing a document.

His advice about writing is modern. What a great thinking thousands of years back!

Jātim kulam sthān vayah shrutāni karma-
artha- sheel- anyath desha kālau;
Yauna anubandham cha samikshya kārye
lekham vidadhyār purush anurupam.

One must mention complete introduction and address like name, place, faith, age, ability, work, wealth, moral character, country, marital status, and relation. In the document the following five things must be maintained:

➤ **Arthakram**: Sequence in meaning; main points and sub points;

➤ **Artha sambandha**: Coherence in meaning; without contradiction;

➤ **Paripurnatā**: Everything entered well; using only meaningful and effective words;

➤ **Mādhurya**: Use of known and common words;

➤ **Spastatā**: Clarity in meaning; using simple, apt and appropriate words

Then he discusses different types of writing and even correctness in *vākya*, sentence, how to write, what to write and what not to write. In this context he lists many weaknesses in writing like *akrānyi; vyāghāt; punarukta; apashabda* and *samplava*. He declares that a letter can have any one or more than one of the following as the subject matter:

Ākhyān: suggestions   *Arthanā*: request
Prasansā: admiration   *Prichchhā*: enquiry

Nindā: blame	*Nishedha*: negation
Pratyākhān: denial	*Upālambha*: complain
Pratishedha: order to stop	*Chodanā*: encouraging
Sāntvanā: consolation	*Abhyupapatti*: readiness to help

It is undoubtedly a great book for people in different business and for those who are controlling a business. One example will be sufficient. In 2:27:11, *Kosha-Pravesha-Ratna-Parikshā*, Kautilya has discussed all the varieties and qualities of not only pearl- and diamond- like jewels, but also of wool. It is something wonderful and unbelievable that during those days people considered such things in such painstaking detail. In the next three–four chapters he has discussed gold, its tests, the duties of the chief gold keeper; how to maintain stock of gold and granary; forests; sale management, etc. It shows his knowledge of trees, furniture wood, diseases, etc., in minute detail.

Panyādhyaksha: Sale Management

Internal Sales

In the chapter 2:32:16, *Panyādhyaksha*, Kautilya has given some hints as insight into sales management. Now it is obvious that most of the subtle techniques of sales management were given by Chānakya and are in vogue since his time. There is hardly any change in it.

The very first instruction deals with the produce from water and land. The sale of goods through waterways and land is a part of it. He suggests first to gather information regarding regularly sold commodities and rarely sold commodity; costly articles, *bahumulya*; and cheap articles, *alpa mulya*; that which the consumers like and purchase, which is in constant demand, *mānga*; and that which the consumers don't like, are disinterested in, and rarely purchase, *aruchikar*. It is a very clear indication that one must know the need and mood of the market if one has to succeed in business:

Panya adhyakshah sthal-jalajānām nānā-vidhānā panyānām sthal
atha vāri patha upāyātānām sār-phalgāarghāntaram
priya-apriyatā cha vidyāt.

He should also collect and keep information ready about the right and ripe time to sell a particular commodity and to buy it; the right time to reduce the stock and to fill the godown: *vikshepa sankshep kraya vikraya prayoga kālān.*

The commodity which is available in abundance should be delicately handled, first the price should be raised to create havoc and when the profit has come then to reduce the price to bring the existing stock to normal:

Yachcha panyam prachuram syātād yekikrity ārgham āropayet.
Prāpte arghe vārghāh anantaram kāryet.

If an article is sold at different places then all the traders should sell it at the same price: *bahumukham wā rāja panyam vaidehakāh kritārgham vikri-niran.*

If the price comes down while in sale then it should be covered up by the traders: *Chheda-anurupam cha vaidharanam dadyuh.*

Import and Export

The products of one's own kingdom should be sold at one particular and fixed place. The produce from other countries should be sold at different places: *swa-bhumija-anām rāja-panyānām-yeka-mukham vyavahāram sthāpayet; par-bhumi jānānām-aneka-mukham.*

The sale of national products and imported articles should be so managed that the citizens are not harassed: *ubhayam cha prajā-nāma-anugrahena vikrāpayet.* It should be immediately stopped if the citizens feel harassed: *sthulam api cha lābham prajā-nāma aupaghātikam vārayet.*

On the stock in store the businessman should pay its 16th part in tax; if the articles being sold are weighed then its 20th part, but if it is to be counted then its 11th part as tax.

There should be some relaxation in the tax on the "imported articles". There should not be any tax on the commodities that are brought by boat or ship. The king should manage loans without interest to foreigners for trade but there should be tax on the persons who are collaborating with foreign traders: *anabhiyogah cha ārthih avāgantunāma anyatra sabhya upakāribhyah.*

In foreign trade, the chief must keep in mind the difference in price of various articles in both the countries; and what will be the net profit after deducting sales tax; border tax; police safety tax; forest safety tax; tax for crossing over the river; and personal expenses.

The businessman should initiate and maintain cordial relations with border-security personnel; city chiefs and powerful personalities to avoid obstacles in trade with another country.

If someone falls deep in trouble in an alien country then one should try one's best to save both the life and jewels but if it is not possible then one should save one's life. One should keep on depositing the tax in a foreign land in time to avoid complications and to establish one's trade: *āpadi sāram ātmanam wā mokshayet. Ātmano wā bhumim prāptah sarva deya vishuddham vyavahāret.*

One should not venture in trade with another country if the way is difficult or dangerous and if there is least profit. In 2:37:21 and 38:22 Kautilya has dealt only with different taxes from road tax to goods tax. In this way, with deliberate planning he has discussed the departments from agriculture to forest; and from gold to cotton, the appointments, income, expenditure, rights, duties, etc.

9

Social Security and Reforms

Chānakya, a young and enthusiastic teacher from Takshasheelā had newly arrived at Pātliputra, the then beautiful capital-city of Magadh Empire. He had come out in the evening to see the markets. It was a neat and clean place with beautiful buildings and well-arranged shops.

When he was engrossed in the aesthetic beauty of sculptor and colours, he heard a cry of help. He looked towards the sound. A woman was being forcibly taken away by two strong men against her will. She was physically protesting and crying for help. He wondered that no one came to her rescue. He moved steadily towards them and asked:

"What is wrong with you? You are pulling the lady as if you are a butcher and she is a goat. Has she cheated you or grabbed your belongings?"

"It's none of your business. Go where you are going. Let us do our job," one of them said.

"And your job is to forcibly pull a shaken and crying lady. Are you sure, you have been appointed for that immoral and unsocial job" Chānakya showed the confidence of a teacher.

"Go away. Don't waste your time and don't teach us morality," the same man said again.

"You need teaching and beating both. It is highly immoral and unethical to grab an unwilling lady. Is she related to you? Is she married to you? Has she taken loans from you? Are you an officer of the court?" Chānakya was bent upon knowing the truth.

The man was very angry: "Go away, otherwise you will be killed."

"On the other hand, I say, free the lady or you will be imprisoned." Chānakya showed greater anger.

Actually, the people passing by don't show interest in a lady being forcibly taken away by someone. But this one was different and a novelty for no one opposed such men. Some people stood there watching the scene and listening to unrealistic words like ethics and morality. They had almost forgotten those words.

The man showed his thick and oiled staff and said: "Go away at once or you will be beaten hard."

"You may not have learnt the lessons well but I teach its practical use to young and strong students. Raise the staff and you will find your head broken." Saying so, Chānakya put the book he had in his hand in the anga vastram, and taking it from his soldiers bound it around his waist and was ready for the fight. He placed his right foot forward in a position of attack.

Both the men exchanged glances with each other and suddenly released the woman. They had realized that the empty handed man knows the way and trick to snatch the staff easily, then he can give them good beating.

Immoral men have least physical power and no will-power, no inner strength to stand against an ethical person.

Rampant Venereal Diseases

On one side, anarchy was loose upon the villages in the whole of Magadh. The people were as arrogant and sensuous as their king. They were not ready to abide by the law. Grabbing and capturing the neighbouring land was rampant. Elopement and rape was rampant. Social order was broken.

On the other hand, prevalent sex diseases had taken menacing form and the people were suffering from it on mass scale.

Chānakya had another experience in a residential area of Pātliputra. He saw a man sitting on the stairs of a verandah spraining and twisting his body in pain. The face was distorted. His body movement had attracted him. While moving towards him, Chānakya tried to think of the intensity of the pain and guess the cause. He had his hunches but was not sure. He went straight to the man and asked politely:

"What has happened to you? Why are you twisting in pain? Why don't you take some medicine?" He asked many questions

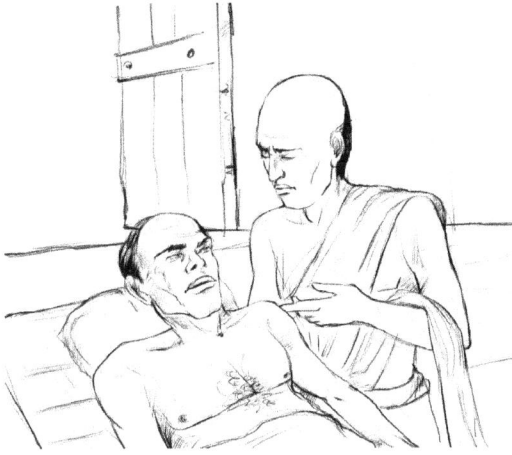

simultaneously. The young man glanced at him and turned his head, then turned his head away but the body showed the pain.

"Don't worry! Tell me. I can help you," he encouraged the young man.

"There is no medicine for it. I am paying the penalty of being heedless. I'm suffering from sujāk, a venereal disease, worse than gonorrhea." The man in intense pain answered looking nowhere in particular thinking of the life wasted.

Chānakya had studied Āyurveda. He knew the cause of the disease. It is uncontrolled physical relation with more than one woman. He immediately prescribed him to boil the leaves of chiraitā, a blood purifier, and to drink the water in which it is boiled.

Chānakya moved ahead but was restless. What is happening here? Why have people no control over themselves or anything else? Why do they indulge in stupid and momentary sensuous pleasure heedless of the consequences?

Appraisal

Control and balance are the keys to success. Nothing can be achieved without control over the self, the situation, the money, matter and man-power. They grow well and lead a happy, healthy and prosperous life who possess control and maintain a balance in almost everything from food to work and sensuous pleasure.

Effect

There is but little space between rise and fall; the steady steps take us up while the shaky and false steps make us fall.

While planning to demolish the Nand Kingdom and in the process of grabbing the palace, Chānakya made many local arrangements and took firm steps for social reforms. When he won then he forced those things with greater vehemence to get rid of the social and personal maladies. He selected wise, sincere and righteous men to solve the problems of limited areas. He started such centres that solved the local problems. His reforms continued. He worked hard for marriages and physical relation with only the spouse. It worked and in a few years the good result encouraged others to get rid of the urge to indulge in sex with many women. Had there not been rampant venereal diseases both men and women have refused to abide by the ethical duties of a spouse after marriage. They had seen the pain and disliked such men. They did not want to be such a patient.

In modern times, people are ready to say goodbye to marriage and make sex free for all. Such days are far away. In the meantime, many have started suffering from different sex diseases including AIDS, the worst among them. It has no cure as the medicine shows no effect on the person suffering from AIDS. It is definitely caused by uncontrolled physical relation with many men or women but to save their face in the society they are telling that it comes from parents; that it is caused by common urinal; that it is infectious. But none can deny that it is invariably caused by sensuous relation with one who is suffering or not clean.

Deeds, Agreements and FIRs

The first two chapters of the third part of the *Kautilya Arthashāstra* deal with different deeds, agreements, FIRs and the judgements.

For the convenience of the citizens particularly the villagers, Chānakya has suggested that there should be three *Dharmastha*, Justice for:

- **Janapada Sandhi**, at the border line of two villages or countries; at the centre of ten villages;
- **Sangrahana** at the centre of ten villages;
- **Drona mukha** at the centre of 400 villages;
- **Sthāniya** at the centre of 800 villages.

He declared all the agreements null and void which were written and signed secretly; inside a house; during the night; in the forest; by force; by deception or in loneliness. Both the parties who enter into the agreement should be punished heavily and the witnesses half of them. But he has exempted all those that live in the forest or work at night or can't come out of the house. If an agreement has been heard by someone not among the parties or witnesses and if it follows the rules then it should be accepted as legal: *parokshena adhi-karna-grahanam-avaktavya-karā wā tirohitā siddha yeshu.*

He has announced judgements also but the most important thing is that the king has to ensure justice to all concerned: both the complainant and defendant. If the king rules righteously he gets the heavenly pleasure but if the king gives pain to his subject then he is never happy. It is a type of binding over the king also to see that his subject is happy, pleased with him and get justice:

> *Rāgyah swa dharmah swargāya prajā dharmena rakshatu;*
> *Arakshitu wā kshep turyā mithyā dandam yato anyathā.*

Anger and Sensuousness

Both anger and sensuousness are weaknesses and derail one from the path of welfare to the path of ruin. The angry and sensuous fail to realize that they are running fast towards complete ruin till they are not ruined completely. Often, they feel that they can control the fall and rise again but both anger and sensuous or any one of the two don't give the relief to regain the lost footing. The fall continues. Both are definitely and always ruinous. Today is the age of anger and illicit sexual relations: parents and children are being killed out of anger; and minor girls are raped and sold for physical pleasure. In both the addictions, concentration is shifted and priorities are changed. The effort has no direction and slowly everything slips out of control.

Between the two, anger is a greater threat because it can be against any one and can show its ugly face anywhere while sensuousness is comparatively secluded. Anger has ruined more persons and families. Yet sensuousness is not far behind.

Those who have anger are destroyed by self anger or the anger of such persons who were hit hard by his anger. People don't prefer to go near an angry fellow. He is easily alienated. They are usually alone. Because of anger, a person easily becomes the enemy and soft target of many. Anger easily creates disasters. The angry are neither loved nor respected, they are hated and neglected.

The sensuous have least time for important works and meeting and directing the others. They are engrossed in their affairs and pleasure. The sensuous are usually destroyed by reduced income, enhanced expense and different diseases. They are not alienated but they prefer to be in selected company and hence are usually with one or none. They are not allowed in inner circle. They are not loved. They are despised and neglected.

When money is lost only the finance is affected but when the number of enemies goes up high the danger against life also increases. The unioin with suffering is very painful. Both anger and sensuousness ruin so it makes hardly any difference which ruins badly and faster and which ruins slowly and painfully. Indeed, slow ruin ultimately gives greater pain in aggregate.

According to Kautilya there are three types of deterioration and ruin in anger, called *"Kopaja Trivarga"*; "anger triangle" and includes: *Vākya Pārushya*, fiery statements; *Artha Dushana*, financial loss, mitigated and pinching meaning; *Danda Pārushya*, unnecessary and excessive punishment. Since, the words pinch and bite deep and last long so *Vākya Pārushya* is more dangerous than the other two.

Kautilya associates *artha dushan*, financial loss caused to others in anger in four ways:

➤ **Adān:** To stop wages despite the completion of work and duty;

➤ **Ādān:** To seize or snatch wealth by punishing others in anger;

➤ **Vināsha:** To destroy wealth out of anger;

➤ **Artha tyāga:** Failing in protecting the wealth because of anger.

According to Kautilya, there are four types of deteriorations in sensuousness, called *Kāma- janya Chaturvarga*, sensuous quadrangle. After a lot of deliberations over them and after trying to declare the worst addictions, he concludes that each of the four are equally harmful though some bring the ruin faster; some only to wealth but some take away health, wealth, virtues, morality and prestige.

➤ **Mrigayā:** Hunting. It is directly dangerous and takes a lot of time. The time, energy and cost is not compensated by the gain which is only superficial and satisfies only lust and ego.

➤ **Dyuta:** Gambling. It is very dangerous as one out of the two is a definite loser. If one gains then the other loses. Moreover, it is give and take of existing wealth. Nothing anew is procured. What is gained through it is lost through it and in the end, it is only loss.

> **Stri**: Woman. Both the gamblers and persons sticking to women care least for other important works. It is not their pastime, it is passion. One fights with another for woman or gambling money.

> **Madirā**: Wine. It affects the very sense, the thinking and thinking process which is always at the root of one's success. The drunkard himself cuts off the root and, as rootless he can't grow, prosper and bloom. There will be no flower or fruit on a rootless plant.

Both anger and sensuousness invite the ruffians and neglect the gentle and wise. Both are full of defects and faults and overpower the addicted person so well that he becomes an emblem of defects and faults. So, both are deadly and ruinous.

Among the angry and sensuous are those persons who have least interest in moral classics and virtuous scriptures. They are ruined who have not studied the classics and scriptures and they are also ruined who have read them but don't follow them. Kautilya advises that one must have patience, serve the old and experienced and control the senses to get rid of the deadly and painful addictions to anger and sensuous pleasure:

Tasmāt kopam cha kāmam cha vyasana ārambham ātmavān;
Parityaja unmool haram vriddha sevi jitendriyah.

Marriage Law, Rights and Heirs

The sixth chapters of his book deal with marriage, rights and share of wife and the heir. He has treated eight types of marriages as legal:

1. **Brāhma Vivāh**: *Kanyā dānam kanyā mangalam kritya brāhmo vivāhah.* When a gentle, humble, wise, ideal, diligent, healthy and impressive groom, who is a good match for the daughter, is selected for her and the marriage is solemnized, it is called **Brāhma vivāh**. The groom's side neither asks for nor gives anything as a precondition to the marriage. The father of the

daughter, however, may give *dāna*, donation; *dahaze*, dowry; *dakshinā*, offerings and *upahār*, gifts.

2. **Daiva Vivāh**: *Antah vedyā amritvije dānād daivah*. When a father chooses and offers his daughter with wealth and ornaments to one of the wise sages, it is called **Daiva vivāh** for it happened by chance and during a *yagya*.

3. **Ārsha Vivāh**: *Gomithunād anād ārshah*. Without any exchange of material things when a marriage and its rituals are performed according to the Scriptures, it is called **Ārsha vivāh**.

4. **Prājāpatya Vivāh**: *Sah-dharma-charyā prājāpatya*. A groom asks for the hand of a marriageable girl in marriage and the father marries them on the condition that they would lead a life of righteousness and follow religious path and live happily together. It is called **Prājāpati vivāh**.

5. **Āsura Vivāh**: *Shulka dānād asurah*. By giving a lot of wealth to the father and family of the groom or to the groom and marrying the daughter to him is called **Āsura vivāh** as it is almost like buying the groom.

6. **Gāndharva Vivāh**: *Mithah samvāyād gāndharvah*. A boy and a girl meet and like each other. They agree to live as a married couple. When they perform marriage at a lonely place or in a lonely temple only by garlanding one another, is known as as **Gāndharva vivāh**.

7. **Rākshasā Vivāh**: *Prasahyād ānād rākshasāh*. To forcibly take away the girl after beating her family members and others and to marry such a girl shaking and weeping out of fear is known as Rākshasā vivāh, the demonic marriage in which there is no human value.

8. **Paishācha Vivāh**: *Supta ādānād paishāchah*. Forcibly making physical relation with a sleeping girl or insane or immature or unconscious girl is called a **Paishāch**

vivāh for the clear reason that such degenerated deeds can be performed only by *pishāch*, the cannibals or the Draculas.

It is wrongly publicised that Hindu woman married or widow has no right of separation or re-marriage. These are wrong notions. Even in the *Manusmriti* there are such provisions on certain conditions. Of course, Kautilya has given more latitude but there are certain conditions that apply.

It is vogue and fashion now to establish business organizations in the name of wives. In that scenario, it is essential to know the rights of women and the ensuing problems about the legal heir. It is essential then to know the traditional facts and current rules. Kautilya has discussed even the state of affairs if a widow remarries. In the case of separation it is up to the husband to see that the wife gets the essential. The financial status of the husband plays an important role. But Kautilya says that if the lady has returned to her parents and is living freely and earning then the husband can't be forced to pay alimony, the allowance for support by one spouse to another.

But if the lady has revolted against the kingdom; has transgressed the moral bindings; become wayward; or got married again, then she has no right for dowry property and alimony:

> *Rāja dvishtā atichārā ābhyām ātma apkramanena cha;*
> *Stri dhana ānit shulkānām swāmyam jāyate striyāh.*

Villages Feed All

For Kautilya, the road to survival and prosperity goes through villages. It is so because all the eatables food products come from the villages. In stark contrast to the emphasis that the *Arthashāstra* assigns to rural development, agriculture, and the textile industry, the status quo in India is that these spheres have been neglected. The demand and lust for infrastructure is so high in the metros and it is spreading fast to villages also that everything essential is being knowingly neglected.

In the sphere of economic administration, India has much to learn from the Kautilya's Arthashāstra, and to follw its ancient, strong, durable and tested path. Kautilya recommends severe penalties on the officials of public enterprises which incurred losses, and rewards for those who showed profits. It is being done in the form of transfer, dismissal or incentives. "Profit" was a "must" in Kautilya's scheme of running a country's administration; and that way any organization and administration because all organizations are a form of governance on a small basis, large scale or very large scale or international scale.

Vāstuke Vāstu Vikrayah: Property Dealing

Property dealing is a very profitable business nowadays. Big corporate houses and builders are in the fray and field. The money is losing its value and the properties are becoming costlier day by day, almost out of the reach of the common folk. Chānakya has dealt with the sale, auction, boundary settlements, taxes, relaxation in tax and punishments for deceptions and excesses.

In an auction, after three hammers, with auctioneer's announcement of 1, 2, 3 the auction and price is declared final. People believe that it is a western style but the fact is that it was started either by Chānakaya or his predecessors in India. They had to call thrice and if there was no further response then the auction was accepted as final. The tradition may have been there but it is first found in the Arthashāstra 3:65:9: *trih āghoshitam vyāhatam kretā kretum labhet*.

The best thing about Chānakya is that he suggests that if someone has to sell out his land or house then first he should ask the neighbours and the *Mukhiyā*. If they refuse then he can talk to outsiders: *gyāti sāmanta dhanikāh kramena bhumi parigrahān kretum- bhyā-bhaveyuh. Tato anye bāhyā.* But ego and jealousy are playing such a treacherous role that people silently and secretly sell their land and house to outsiders.

The other very important thing Chānakya says about: No tax should be taken if someone invests in a new reservoir or renovates old one or extemds it for five, four or three years respectively: *Tatāk setu bandhānām nav pravartane pāncha varshikah prihārah.*

Yet another important aspect is the way he forces the law and discipline. A powerful person in a village can take water for irrigation out of turn, or stops water for others. He announces punishment for such acts:

> *Setubhyo munchastah toyamvāre shat pano damah;*
> *Vāre wā toyam anyeshām pramādena uprundhatah.*

He moves on to discuss the management of ways, villages, meadows, land management, community works and loan and interest and also mortgage. He has announced different interest rate for different business and different places. He says that generally 1.25% interest should be taken but 5% from the businessmen; 10% from the persons who live in forests or do business there and 20% from the persons who do business through seas:

> *Sapād panā dharmyā māsavriddhih pana shatasya.*
> *Panchapanā vyavahāriki.*
> *Dasha panā kāntāragānām.*
> *Vinshati panā sāmudrānām.*

Wholesale and Retail

In 3:68:12, entitled *Aupanidhikam*, Kautilya has dealt with retail and wholesale and the relationship between the retailer and wholesaler along with many other things like mortgage. He has proposed interest to be paid by the retailers on the credit given by the wholesalers but gives relief if the price comes down before the stock is sold out. He gives relief even for breakage or damage in transportation, etc.

He has devised and explained many ways to test the honesty and punish the dishonest traders, and has preferred all the dealings before witnesses:

Tasmāt sākshim adachchhannam kuryāt samyag vibhāshitam;
Swe pare wā jane kāryam desha kāla agra varnatah.

D s- Karma-Kar-Kalpam: Labour Law

Chānakya is dead against the sale as slave of the Aryans and has announced punishment if anyone including a family members sells a minor, *shudra, vaishya, kshatriya* or *brāhmin*. He has no objection if a *"malechchha"* is sold as a slave but declares that an Aryan can't be enslaved at any rate:

Malechchhānām adoshah prajām vikretum ādhātum wā.
Na tveva āryasya dāsa bhāvah.

The employment must be declared and the wages must be paid as agreed. He has discussed and finalized the fee for professionsl but mostly based on the type of work done by them. The wages or fees are to be fixed according to the work done. He proceeds on to discuss in detail the rules for employment; the salary and the employee-employer relationship.

In *Vikrita Krita Anushayah*, he deals with advance payments and punishments to erring persons or parties. He also deals with the sale and purchase of animals and at the close warns the Judges to be just in credit and debit and also in sale and purschase so that no loss is incurred to any one:

Dātā pratigrihitā cha syātām na upahatau;
Dāne kraye wā anushayam tathā kuryuh sabhāsadah.

It has to be given due importance that all the time, Chānakya is conscious of righteousness and has mentioned time and again that unrighteous deeds will destroy the king or even the kingdom. Here too, he concludes that if religious deeds are forcibly suppressed or if the religious deeds are neglected, then the king is ruined: *Dharmo hya adharmo apahatah shāstāram hantya upekshitah*. It is an advice to all to be righteous, moral and ethical and to do only wholesome and meritorious deeds for the welfare and prosperity of self, family, society and the living beings. We can't survive after neglecting religion and our duties towards Nature and other living beings as our survival depends not on us but on others.

That huminity is behind the thinking of Chānakya that he has written one complete chapter (3:75:18) over rough behaviour towards others and has announced punishment for abusing a lame, a dumb, a deaf, a beggar, a blind or handicapped. No one can make a joke of religion, caste or faith; not even of foololishness or wisdom; neither of anyone's profession nor of one's place: residence, village, region or country. He has divided the misbehaviour in five categories: towards *Sharira*, physical deformity; against *prakriti*, nature; with *Shruta*, words; of *Vritti*, profession or of *Desha*, place. He was against the abuse towards a living place or religious place:

Swadesha grāmayoh purvam madhyam jāti sanghayoh;
Ākrosha āda deva chaityānām uttamam dandam arhati.

Agreements: Marriage and Heirs

A whole *Adhikaran* deals with agreements, punishments, marriage and wealth for woman; heirs; judgements on in-fights in villages for land, house and crops, etc; loans and interest; mortgage; employees and employers; buying and selling of minors and women; fixing salary and remuneration; advance for sale and purchase; property and ownership. These are all related to well or ill-manged property and affairs. Chānakya had shown the way.

The topics mentioned above are mostly related to the management of movable and immovable property, its disputes and decisions. But loans and interest and budgets are directly related to business and corporate world where maximum of business are running on credits and loans and most of the organizations are paying huge interest every month.

Unlike in Kautilya's state where the king was accessible to his people every day at least for one and a half hours, in India today it takes a long time even to get a "hearing." Some of the ground rules and measures suggested in the *Arthashāstra*, particularly those which pertain to matters relating to budget, accounts and audit, are applicable to present day India. In Kautilya's state, the king could severely punish the corrupt officials, however highly they were placed. In India, those in political office are rarely convicted even if they are corrupt or proved guilty of committing certain offences.

Kautilya clearly states that the management should be such that neither the loaner nor the seeker; neither the seller nor the purchaser is the loser:

Dātā pratigrahitā cha shyātām na upahatau yathā;
Dāne kraye wā anushayam tathā kuryuh sabhāsadah.

The official must work sincerely and without prejudice:

Yevam kāryāni dharmasthāh kuryuh achhala- darshinah;
Samāh sarveshu bhāveshu vishwāsyā loka- sampriyāh.

10

Steady Economy

Chānakya invented and employed many methods to keep the flow of deposits to the treasure and to restrict the withdrawl to the most needed. He did not like wastage of anything: energy, time, money, skill, wisdom, and knowledge, and of course, resources. The resources should never dry out. If dried, it would spell doom.

Chief Executives and their Salary

Kautilya has divided chief executives into three categories, and fixed their salary: 48,000 *panas* per annum to the first category; just half, 24,000 *panas* per annum for the second category, and again the half of it 12,000 *panas* per annum for the third category. The following are the three categories:

First Category

> *Mantri*: Minister;
> *Purohit*: Chief Executive;
> *Senāpati*: Chief of Army;
> *Yuvarāja*: Prince;

Second Category

> *Dauvārika*: Chief of the palace;
> *Antavanshika*: Chief of domestic affairs;

- *Prashāstri* or *Prashāstā*: Chief of Prisons;
- *Samāhartā*: Chief of all stores;
- *Sannidhātā*: Chief of Treasure;

Third Category

- *Pradeshtā*: Chief of Public Relations;
- *Nāyak*: Chief of a section of the Army;
- *Paur*: Chief Administrative Officer of the capital city;
- *Vyāvāhārika*: Chief Justice;
- *Kārmātika*: Chief of Mines;
- *Sabhya*: Chairman of the Council of Ministers;
- *Dandapāl*: Chief Civil Officer of Army;
- *Antapāl* or *Rāshtrāntpāl*: Chief of the Frontiers;
- *Durgapāl*: Chief of Defense

Steady economy has become a dream which was a fact some four decades ago. In the earlier chapter, Kautilya had identified several areas of State intervention to facilitate the economic life of the country. They are as follows:

- The superintendent of slaughterhouse
- The superintendent of prostitutes
- The superintendent of ships
- The superintendent of passports
- The office of the city superintendent

Kautilya's idea of the Passport corresponds to the modern version of this document that facilitates movement of people. This is perhaps the first instance of an institutionalized concept of passports that regulate the flow of people across borders.

Kautilya said that "whoever is provided with a pass shall be at liberty to enter or go out of the country."

Fixation of Salary from Top to Bottom

In 5:91:3, *Bhritya Bharaniyam*, Kautilya has fixed the salary for each of the employees in different cadre and for different work. The salary is given in *Pana*, the money in vogue at that time. But there is a general trend. He has fixed a salary for the highest cadre and the next higher cadre will get half of the salary of first grade; and the next cadre half of the salary of the second grade and so on. It can be understood like this: $A=A$; $B=A/2$; $C=B/2$; $D=C/2$; $E=D/2$, and so on.

He put stress on the fostering and security of the employees and their family. It is up to the managing authorities, the officials in particular but the governance and the king in general to ensure the security and safety of body and rights of the citizens or the employees.

In the same way, very heavy punishment should be given to the employees, whosoever, he/she may be if he/she tries to deceive in any way.

Kautilya realized that the role of the State was to ensure that commercial activities do not violate laws or are harmful for the consumer and if the State did not establish and enforce codes of conduct, it would, in fact, raise transaction costs. The lack of trust and guarantee of quality would diminish commerce and increase search and verification costs for agents undertaking commercial transactions.

Anujivi Vritam: Employees Behaviour towards Employer

An employee must lay certain conditions before the employer. Boldly tell your boss before appointment:

- "Such persons should not be asked to assess me or pass comments on my deeds and words who have no intelligence and are not versed in religious and moral teachings."

- "You won't indulge in fight or competetion against a powerful person or against someone who has powerful adviser".

- "I must not be punished at sudden anger or rush of blood".

- "The conditions of my appointments should not be made public".

- "You must honour my advice when I symbolically warn you".

- "These conditions must be fulfilled".

- Kautilya has some sacred suggestions for the employees. The employees must keep them in mind and must follow them.

- One should accept employment only with an *ātma sampanna*, self organized Boss, with or without wise counselors.

- Maintain a reasonable distance from the Boss. Be neither very close nor very far away.

- Never blame the Boss; never behave with him in uncivilized manner; never tell a lie; and never narrate unbelievable incidents.

- Do not speak in loud voice. Don't clear throat or cough while speaking.

- Don't speak to him in the presence of a person of equal status.

- Don't either accept or refuse a scandal.

- Don't behave like the Boss or like a cheat.
- Don't wink in his presence.
- Don't show strain or consternation.
- Don't fall in dispute with his relatives, ladies or near and dear ones of ladies.
- Don't create relationship with his enemies.
- Don't repeat the same thing many times.
- Don't make a group among employees.
- Inform him immediately if something is really very important.
- Neither be a sycophant nor a backbiter.
- Don't pass information regarding colleagues.
- If you need favour, don't tell directly. Pass it on through someone close to your Boss.
- If you need favour for others, say it at the right time in right manner.
- Talk only which is righteous and necessary for prosperity:

    Aheen kālam rājārtham swārtham priya hitaih sah;
    Parārtham desha kāle cha bruyād dharma artha sanghitam.

- With his permission, you can say something favourable, even if it is not sweet.
- Don't say anything unfavourable or bitter truth.

    Prishtah priya hitam bruyānna bruyād hitam priyam;
    Apriyam wā hitam bruyāchchhrinvato anumato mithah.

- When the Boss laughs, laugh pleasantly but never loudly.
- Keep silence if afraid of telling the truth.

- Don't say yourself but send a message regarding disgusting news.

- If some responsibility befalls forgive, and endure its result.

- Be careful. The master can destroy you and your family or can make you prosperous.

Then in the next chapter *Samaya Chārikam*, Kautilya makes it clear how one can know whether the master is pleased or angry. He has given the reasons in minute detail which is important for those that have their work with or around their master.

11

Pragmatic Approach

Throughout his life, Chānakya tried to achieve balance by controlling his anger and emotions but all the time he found himself on this extreme or that extreme. This made him more determined to search out a balancing point in everything that came before him. He tried to see the incidents with a detached view but his ego overruled the balancing factors and guided him to take extreme steps. He too knew that his task was not that of a householder leading a social and family life. How can one think of being balanced when there is war looming large, and conspiracy taking place at many places for different things and with cunning aims? He had to give proper answer which was definitely retaliation in battles and nipping the conspiracies while a bud.

It is one great reason that barring the heads of the organizations, he has taught balanced view and action for all else. Even for the heads of the states or organization he has suggested to collect and keep information and weigh the proofs before taking the final decision.

To the best of his abilities, Chānakya also tried to delay the matters and think in a balanced way. This gave him a wider scope, to gauge both ends, the edges and the centre. As a result, Chānakya was everywhere. He was so effective that no one dared to ignore him. Even in modern context, those who will read, understand and follow him will never get defeated. A very happy and prosperous life is ensured for those who achieve balance in life, i.e. in everything from personal to universal; from family to international; from material to spiritual and from outer to inner.

Chānakya is practical in his aphorisms, dictums and political and economic thoughts. He is the single person who has written almost everything with his own experiences. When he seems to be quoting someone else then it is guaranteed that he has tested that statement. Otherwise, in the whole of the *Arthashāstra* he has given opposite views and refused to budge to the ideas of great Sages like Manu; Brihaspati; Shukra and Nārada, etc.

Chānakya was not headstrong. He accepted everything pragmatic and worth following. He used to move from place to place collecting information and passing orders. In that process, he saw many extraordinary things and had some such experiences.

After raising an army and declaring Chandragupta as the Samrāt, Chānakaya started attacking the Magadha capital and was readily defeated. He was worried. He could not find flaw in his thinking and planning yet the success eluded him. Why? He was worried but one day, an old widow provided him the reason mix the answer. Accordingly he changed his tactics and started getting success. That incident is an eye-opener, hence it is being described below.

A Practical Suggestion

In three different ways and occasions Chānakya attacked Magadh under the leadership of Chandragupta and every time he was defeated. He was desolate. He was unable to pinpoint the mistake. The worried Chānakya was mentally taxed and paying heavy interest.

Customarily, he would loiter during the night to take stock of the situation and to keep an eye over the happenings. One late night, when he was passing through a village, he saw light coming out from a hut. He automatically turned towards it. There were many small holes in the hut and it was easy to see all that was happening inside.

From their talk Chānakya gathered that the hut belonged to a widow. She had a son. She had brought some grain late in the evening. She had laboured hard for hours to change it into flour and then was able to cook the meal.

When the boy started eating he tried to take a morsel from the middle and in the process burnt his fingers. (In another version he took a bite from the middle of bread.) In either case the mother was angry.

"You fool! You're behaving like Chānakya who is attacking at the centre. Food is never eaten from the centre. It's always eaten from a side." The angry old woman taught an important lesson.

Chānakya heard it and was amazed as the practical suggestion was like a boon to him. He thought over it for a long time, realized his mistake and returned satisfied and confident. It's needless to state that from there on he started attacking the kingdom at the boundary. Maharājā Ghanānand was not able to send his army in time and started losing one controlling centre after another. Chandragupta won every such smaller kingdom. There was no dearth of wealth and army. Enriched and encouraged by such small victories Chānakya prepared a practical plan and gave the final blow and won the biggest and richest kingdom of Magadh.

Appraisal

In marketing, it is not wise to attack the stronghold of the established competitor, neither the market that gives him the best business nor its long standing dealers. It is always better to attack and crack to make an opening by taking under control the sporadic markets.

Commodity, Roads and Infrastructure

Kahān aur Kaisā Vyāpār?

Where and which Commodity?

For investment in bridges and canals, it is better to invest near the agricultural land. It is more useful throughout the year.

For further invest, it is better to invest in forests and orchards with fruit trees and flowers. It is more benefial for its every part is useful.

Investment in utility goods is better than costlier and luxurious goods as there are few customers for it.

Invest in the commodity that needs least investmenmt and offers greater gain.

Investment in infrastructure means blocking the money. It loses value and even destroyed after a few decades.

It is better to invest in greater number of animals than in big and powerful animals.

> For business, the land route is far better than water route:

> As on land path there are many cities for trade;

> The land route can't be seized from every direction;

> It is available in every season;

> It is less dangerous than water route.

> The road leading to north is better for its population and trade centres.

> That path is better in which there are mines.

Kautilya talks of definite understanding on the basis of investment, effort, sale and dividend. Many organization come to an understanding about the zones; some on product; some on particular big customer; some on the quality of product; and many sell the products of other organizations in their area and vice versa.

Kautilya further talks of the ways to be strong and raise resources in the chapter *Heena shakti puranam*:

> To take the advice of elders, learned and experienced;

> To keep the relation cordial with the subject for they give money, soldiers, and arms and enrich the centre. It is like keeping cordial relation with the Distributors and Dealers.

> To get canals and reservoirs for the growth of agricultural production.

To open roads up to the enemy territory;

> To take care of mines;

> To take care of forests;

> To collect and befriend the enemies of the enemy.

By following these ways the weak king can keep on facing the opponents; the growing organization can survive and prosper:

Yevam pakshena mantrena dravyena cha balena cha;
Samapannah prati nirgachchhet par avagraham ātmana.

Collecting and Experiencing News and Views

Chānakya is the first person to analyze, theorize and lay principles for all these and many more activities; and hence, he is accepted globally as the first management guru. He was the first to point out that the success of a person lies in looking well after each activity connected to him, and in the handling of all the men employed and materials used. He knew and has discussed in length in *Kautilya Arthashāstra* that management is goal oriented and a group activity, which depends on work culture and environment and on keeping all the threads connected well and working efficiently.

Of course, this short of industrialization was not established or even invented during or from before his time, but there were industries and variety of things were produced at a large scale and international business among many countries was in vogue.

As Chānakya had to destroy an empire so he had to collect information in detail about the departments and functions; and as the head of a rising empire he had to arrange everything afresh and make the administration tidy and efficient. He succeeded in everything that he did, because:

➤ He knew the art and science of formally organizing groups, creating environment, encouraging people to work harder and getting the things done.

➤ He has the knowledge and ability of subtracting the maximum with minimum effort and investment.

➤ He knew planning, organizing, commanding and controlling, coordinating and achieving both the immediate and long-term gains.

➤ He knew "exactly" what he has in mind, what was he going to do, what were his requirements, from where they could be fulfilled and "exactly" how the goal could be achieved.

12

Taking over Organizations

Before demolishing the Nand dynasty and killing the king, queen and their kiths and kins, Chānakya had only their destruction in mind but once the vow was fulfilled and the said destruction took place, he immediately switched over to consolidating the Maurya dynasty by uniting India. He tried hard in this direction and employed all the ploughs and shot all the arrows that he knew and that looked to be sure shot.

Marriages of Chandragupta for Grabbing Kingdoms

Chānakya thought of the welfare of the nation. India was passing through a critical phase. It was a period of transition. He wanted the security to the country and safety to its people. Greeks were still there. Alexander had returned. He had appointed Seleucus Nicator to govern India. Chānakya was looking out a way to make him friend and grab the kingdom which was still under his control. He knew well about his daughter Helen, also known as Cornelia. He planned the marriage of Chandragupta with Helen.

He announced his decision to his dear pupil and king. Chandragupta was in a fix. He was not in a position to deny his mentor but he secretly loved a girl named Chitrā. He wanted to marry her. He was looking for an opportune moment to declare his intention. Chānkya knew everything. He had planned everything. He had to consolidate the position. Chandragupta got the opportunity and declared his love and willingness to marry Chitrā. Chānakya was not lenient. He did

not listen to the king and forced him to marry Cornelia. The king had to surrender to his Guru.

In all probability the marriage was solemnized in 305 BC, when Seleucus Nicator was defeated in the battle. As dowry and as the defeated general, he gave four big provinces to Chānakya. They were Kabul, Kandhār, Herāt and Makarān. Appius has described the war. Other details are available in Indica written by Megasthenese.

Chānakya did not stop here. He had yet another kingdom in his eyes. The king had only a daughter named Durdha. He was sure to get that kingdom in dowry. He announced marriage to be performed. Again Chandragupta opposed and again Chānakya silenced him saying that lesser things are sacrificed for greater gains. The king surrendered and the marriage was solemnized.

It's also claimed that later on Chandragupta married Chitrā. He informed Chānakya that he has promised Chitrā to marry her and despite two marriages she is hopeful and waiting for him. (This theme has been dramatically and poetically given the form of a play entitled Chandragupta by Jaishankar Prasad, a famous poet and dramatist of Hindi.) By then his mission was almost finished so Chānakya did not oppose that marriage. He got it performed as he had done the others.

In India, marriages are treated as sacred and are performed to last till the death; so, relations created by marriages are also lasting. Marriage was the most lasting seal on the treaties. It is true in business partnerships also and has been in vogue from time immemorial. Business and corporate houses have preferred marriage relations to establish partnerships.

Effect

Business relations and partnerships must last for mutual faith; overall growth and steady rise.

Labdha Prashanam: Taking Over an Organization

When one takes over an organization three conditions arise. It may be *nava lābh*, fresh gain; it may be *bhuta purva lābha*, own lost organization; or *pitraya lābha*, it may be own organization lost by father or forefathers. After gaining or regaining, some precautions are to be taken:

➤ **Nava Lābha**: In all the cases, the faith of the employees must be won over. In new gain, the CEO, MD, or Director, must do something extra and righteous to establish that he is far superior to the earlier Chief. The qualities of the ex-Chief should be overwhelmingly replaced by the qualities of the new Chief. He must do some righteous and meritorious deeds; show sympathy and compassion; and put in the mind of the employees that he is a better judge of the situation and a far superior and kind administrator. He should show interest in social, political, religious and organizational meetings and congregations.

➤ **Purva Lābha**: When one regains one's lost organization then he should never repeat the mistakes that he committed earlier. He must get rid of all his faults, defects and ignorance. He must enrich the qualities which helped him regain the organization.

➤ **Pitraya Lābha:** If some faults in his father caused the loss then it is up to the son who has regained it to hide the faults and mistakes and advertise well the good qualities that the father or forefathers possessed.

In all the three cases, the new Chief must follow the good qualities that were lacking in that organization. He must encourage the religious, righteous, and ethical persons. He should never allow the unrighteous, non-religious and unethical deeds and ideas germinate in that organization. He must stop the entry of non-religious and deceptive persons:

Charitram akritam dharmyam kritam cha anyaih pravartyet;
Pravartyenna cha dharmyam kritam cha anyaih nivartayet.

One thing must be marked and taken into consideration about Chānakya that he seems to be at the extreme end of destruction and at the extreme end of creation and re-establishment as well, but his aim is always to achieve a balance between the two edges, two extremes. He leads the best life who lives a balanced life trying to achieve greatness in all the four pursuits; not in one, two or three.

Theories and Practise

Chānakya used and utilized all the *Nities*: ways and methods, to take over other kingdoms. He used them all: Fear, Illusion, Killing, Divisions, Lust and Battles for grabbing other kingdoms. He kept on doing it till India was not a united whole. The Kingdom spread from this end, North to that end, South.

As a result of his efforts, the Maurya Empire had smooth administration and efficient ruler. The government was hierarchical and centralized with lot of staff to make sure that work was carried on smoothly and efficiently. Taxes were collected regularly, trade and commerce was carried on smoothly, citizens were taken care of and the army was always ready for any sort of external aggression or threat. Every province had its own officials who managed administration at grassroots level. The economy was agrarian and the main economic activity of people was agriculture. Pātliputra, the capital city of Magadh was beautifully decorated and had all facilities that any modern city would have.

In the Mauryan dynasty, art and literature flourished and the rulers built many famous temples and monuments. They followed the rules and concepts laid down great advisor Chānakya, who remained the driving force behind the fame and success of Emperor Chandragupta. For making his ideas available for the posterity chānakya wrote many great books that have been regarded as masterpieces.

Known as the founder of the Mauryan Empire, King Chandragupta Maurya is still considered to be the most authentic and able rulers of India, and Chānakya as the wizard who single handedly demolished a kingdom and acquired power and resources to establish another far greater and stable empire. The following are some of his concepts expressed in the *Arthshāstra* on take over, security, expansion and treaties, etc:

> ➤ "The welfare of a state depends on an active foreign policy." 6:2:1.

> ➤ "An enemy's destruction shall be brought about even at the cost of great losses in men, material and wealth." 7.13.33.

> ➤ "A king weak in power shall endeavor to promote the welfare of his people. For power comes from the countryside, which is the source of all activities.". 7:14:18-19

> ➤ "One should never submit spinelessly, not sacrifice oneself in fool hardly valour. It is better to adopt such policies as would enable one to survive and live to fight another day." 7.15.13-20,12.1.1-9.

Foreign Policy

➤ "The king shall develop his state, i.e. augment his resources and power for him to embark on a conquest." What it meant that a prosperous state which looked after its people had high rates of economic growth and then the army is always ready to undertake military conquests.

➤ "The enemy shall be eliminated."

➤ "Those who help are friends."

➤ "Peace is to be preferred to war."

➤ "The king's behaviour, in victory and defeat, must be just."

➤ "A small revolt in the rear outweighs a large gain at the front"

➤ "A prudent course shall always be adopted." One has to be practical, be guarded against spineless submission and foolhardy valour.

➤ Kautilya opines that peace can be made with enemy, purely as a temporary measure, provided it gives time to the conqueror to build up strength before conquering the enemy.

➤ "Any activity which harms the progress of the enemy engaged in similar undertakings is also progress."

Setting out on a Campaign

➤ "After the king has increased his strength he shall set out on a campaign against the enemy, choosing a time when the enemy does not have all his forces mobilized." 7.4.14.

➤ "He shall set out on a campaign when he finds that the enemy's troubles with one constituent of his state cannot be compensated by the other constituents, the enemy's subjects have become impoverished, disunited due to oppression by the troops or ill-treatment by their monarch and thus have become susceptible to enticement to desert." 7.4.15.

➤ "Non-intervention, negotiating a peace treaty and making peace by giving a hostage – all mean the same thing, since the aim of all three is to create confidence between the two kings." 7.17.1-2.

➤ "A weak king, attacked by a stronger king whose armies had already started moving against him, shall quickly submit for peace with the offer of himself, his army, treasury and territory." 7.3.22.

➤ "The hostage shall liberate himself by his own efforts or be helped by clandestine agents adopting various disguises." 7.17.33.52.

Choice of Allies

➤ "When there is a choice between two allies, the one amenable to control, though temporary is preferred because he remains an ally as long as he helps. The real characteristic of friendship is help". 7.9.9-12.

➤ "The constant ally giving small help shall be preferred. The temporary friend giving substantial help is likely to withdraw for fear of having to give more or will expect it to be repaid. The constant ally, giving small help continuously, does in fact give great help over a period of time". 7.9.13-17.

➤ "An ally mobilizing quickly, even if he is less mighty, is preferable because he does not allow opportune time for action to pass." (7.9.18-21)

➤ "Troops that are in one place can be brought under control by conciliation or other means." (7.9.22-25).

➤ "An ally who helps monetarily is preferable because one can always use money but troops only sometimes." (7.9.26-30).

➤ "An ally who is likely to grow in power after defeating the enemy and thus become uncontrollable shall be embroiled in a conflict with his own neighbour or such actions would be taken as would oblige the ally to remain obedience, in return for the help received". (7.18.).

13

Treaties

In the *Arthashāstra* Chānakya had written all the practical aspects of dealing with other kings or organizations. He held the opinion that any treaty is not eternal. One can enter into a treaty when needed and break away from it when one is strong enough. Treaties must be always for gain this way or that way.

Signing on and breaking away from Treaties

When Chānakya had won a few battles at borders and started the Maurya dynasty, the Kingdom of King Parvat Rāja was at a strategic point. Once, he thought of attacking him but it was not his aim to defeat a small kingdom. He was interested in snatching Magadh from the hands of Ghanānand. He collected information regarding the social, political and economic condition of King Parvat Rāja and then fixed a meeting with him.

He met him along with Chandragupta and the Army Chief Bhadrabhatt. He laid down his position and propositions. Parvat Rāja thought well before coming to a conclusion. He was in between the two. After considering the propositions well Parvat Rāja agreed and a treaty was signed for mutual help and no attack on each other. It was also agreed that the army will move without obstruction through his land.

A few years passed, Maurya dynasty was established. Many small kingdoms either voluntarily became a part of the new Empire or were attacked and won over. The presence of King Parvat Rāja was pinching Chānakya as he was in an important route. He decided to capture it.

Chānakya broke the treaty on the pretext of the higher and difficult demands of Parvat Rāja. He then waited patiently for six months. He knew the weaknesses of the king and laid a net accordingly. The king failed to read the unwritten message of the attack. So, after six months when the Mauryan Army attacked, he was taken aback.

He fought with an unprepared Army against the well trained, versed and prepared Army that outnumbered his army and outwitted in every strategy and at strategic point. Chandragupta won and his the kingdom became a part of the Maurya Empire.

Appraisal

Before planning to take over a business empire one must study the pros and cons and calculate the overall gain. When it seems that the takeover will enhance the overall value and subsequent gain then one should meticulously make preparations, weaken that organization and takeover cheaply. It will be difficult to recover higher price as sale will have to be re-doubled which is not possible immediately.

Effect

The knowledge of the market, consumer's need and usefulness of the products decide the fate of an organization.

Ākramana aur Sandhi: Attack or Treaty

Some claim that there are only two main qualities: *Sandhi wā bigrah;* friendship or enmity; treaty or fight but Kautilya has listed six in the chapter entitled *Shād gunya samudeshah,* the first chapter of part seven, as discussed above.

> *Par smāddhiya mānah sandadhita.*

> *Abhyuchiya māno vigraniyāt.*

> *Na mām paro nā aham param upahantum shakta itya āsit.*

> *Guna atishaya yukto yāyāt.*

> *Shaktiheenah sanshrayet.*

> *Sahāya sādhye kārye dvaidhi bhāvam gachchhet.*

> *Sandhi:* Treaty; the friendship between two on certain grounds;

> *Samān:* Neutral, neither treaty nor enmity;

> *Bigrah:* Separation; to bring harm to another;

> *Āsana:* To show utter disregard;

> *Yāna:* To attack on another;

> *Dvaidhibhāva:* Dual policy; treaty when needed and harm when there is an opportunity.

The central organization or a growing organization can forget reducing the enemy to "not" and concentrate on its own prosperity by following the above mentioned six definite and tested ways:

> *Yevam shadbhih gunaih ywtaih sthitah prakriti mandale;*
> *Paryeshet kshayāt sthānam sthānād vriddhim cha karmasu.*

Treaty for Trade

These qualities have been explained in detail in the subsequent chapters. Then three types of battle are given called: *Prakāsh Yuddha; Kuta Yuddha; Tushni Yuddha.* But the head of an institution has some pious duties towards those that help during rough weather. If one gets equal share then *Sandhi;* if less then *Bigrah;* if more then *vishishta.* One should maintain the relation according to *lābhānsha*, dividend. Without doubt, these things are still in vogue in political, social and business circle. Sometimes, the relation is maintained not on gain or dividend but the value of total sale in a fiscal year.

Kautilya considered trade the third pillar of economic activity and in consonance with this the *Arthashāstra* details every aspect of trade. For instance, apart from promoting trade by improving infrastructure, the state was required to keep trade routes free of harassment by courtiers, state officials, thieves, and frontier guards. Kautilya appears to mistrust traders believing them to be thieves, with a propensity to from cartels to fix prices and make excessive profits as also to deal in stolen property. He prescribed heavy fines for discouraging such offences by traders and with a view to consumer protection. Further, the law on dealings among private merchants included:

> Selling on agency basis.

> Revocation of contracts between traders.

> Traders traveling together and pooling their goods.

> Safety of goods in transit

Sandhi: Conditions for Collaborations

The insight and depth of Chānakya or Kautilya can't be measured or fathomed. The example of 7:101-102: 3: chapter on treaty entitles *Samaheena Jyāyasā Guna Abhinivesho Heena Sandhayah Cha*; is enough to feel that. In it he has distinguished one type of treaty with another and name more than a dozen treaties. These can be easily compared to or understood as collaboration or conditions for collaborations and akin to modern day franchise which is more in vogue now. If one is conscious, diligent and wise one can destroy the parent body or take over that organization while obviously collaborating. The ways are the following.

> **Amisha Sandhi:** When the weak and defeated king surrenders after taking army and wealth from the victor, it is called *Amisha Sandhi*.

> **Purushāntar Sandhi**: When the Commander and the Prince are given to the victorious, it is called *Purushāntar Sandhi*. It is also called *Ātma Rakshana Sandhi*, Self Protecting Treaty.

> **Adrishta Purusha Sandhi**: When a treaty is entered on the condition that either the army will be sent or the king will go alone then it is called *Adrishta Purusha Sandhi*. It is also called danda *Mukhya Ātma Rakshana* as the king and the higher authorities in army are saved.

> **Danda Upanat Sandhi**: When the powerful organization enters marital relation and controls others through slow poison, etc, it is called *Danda Upanat Sandhi*.

> **Parikraya Sandhi**: When money is paid for the release of arrested ministers, etc, it is called *Parikraya Sandhi*; and if this treaty is entered into on the condition of the payment of money in installments, then it is called **Upagraha Sandhi**, and when the time and place of insrtalments are fixed, then it is called **Pratyaya Sandhi**.

> **Kanyādāna Sandhi**: When the agreed money is paid in time, it is called *Kanyādāna Sandhi*. Since, money is paid in it, so it is also called *Suvarna Sandhi*.

> **Kapāla Sandhi**: When there is the provisions that the money is to be paid immediately then it is called *Kapāla Sandhi* but this *Durabhi Sandhi* has no place in the Classical Treatises. When the horses and elephants are given then they are so poisoned that they die at the new king within a week.

> **Koshopanat Sandhi**: In the treaties mentioned earlier the first instalment is paid and then the other payments are postponed on this or that pretext then it is called *Koshopanat sandhi*.

> **Ādishta Sandhi**: For saving the kingdom and the land when a treaty is entered after giving a part of the land, it is called *Ādishta Sandhi*. After some time, the citizens living in that land are encouraged to declared revolt

against their new boss. In nationalizations, the merged employees created a lot of problem which got pacified only after their retirement or death.

➢ **Uchchhinna Sandhi**: In a treaty, when unfertile and almost uninhabited land is given, then it is called *Uchchhinna Sandhi*. That king waits for some calamity to befall on the victorious king that may give him an opportunity to re-take and re-capture the given land.

➢ **Apakraya Sandhi**: In the treaty in which the produce is given and the land is taken back, is called *Apakraya Sandhi*. When something more is given along with the produce, then it is **Para Dushan Sandhi**.

In these types of treaties land is given, so these are also called *Abaliyasa Sandhi* or *Bhumi Upanat sandhi* or *Desha Upanat Sandhi*.

Among all these treaties, *Danda Upanat, Kosha Upanat* and *Desha Upanat* are ordinary treaties and hence, should be used wisely according to the need of time, place and enemy for own advantages.

In 7:111:6, Kautilya discusses *Sandhi* in different way and context. He divides treaties in two:

➢ **Paripanita sandhi**: In Paripanita Sandhi the condition of time, place and action are decided and laid there in.

➢ **Aparipanita Sandhi**: In Aparipanit Sandhi there is no condition of time, place and action. It is done only to become faithful and to know the weaknesses, and also to make the other weaker. When these things are accomplished then to attack and win.

➢ **Prakāsh Yuddha**: Kautilya has divided war, hostility, conflict, monopoly war, marketing tactics, ad-compaign in three divisions. When a war is announced against a country or orgamization, it is called **Prakāsh Yuddha**. In reality and even in corporate world such open battles are rare.

➢ **Kuta Yuddha**: When little strength is shown to be abundance to create fear or small sale is advertised as record sale to lure the competitor for different gains through **Kuta Yuddha** which is fought secretly.

➤ **Tushni Yuddha:** When an enemy or a competitor is destroyed with the help of hired agents, killers, criminals and secret agents then it is called **Tushni Yuddha.**

➤ Again in 7:115:9, Kautilya discusses **Mitra Sandhi** and **Hiranya Sandhi**; and goes on discussing **Sama Sandhi**, **Visham Sandhi** and **Ati Sandhi** and then treaties related to land.

Mitra Guna: Characteristics of Friends

In 7:115:9, Chānakya has placed friendhip as the topic of discussion, analysis and conclusions. Like treaty, he has depicted friendhip in detail and has presented different facets of friendship including the real and opportunistic friends. According to qualities, Chānakya has divided friends into six groups:

Nityam vashyam lahjutthānam pitri paitāmaham mahat;
Advaidhyam cha iti sampannam mitram shad guunam uchyate.

➤ **Nitya Mitra:** Out of love and long relationship one helps the other then they are *nitya mitra.*

➤ **Vashya Mitra:** There are three types of **Vashya Mitra.** One who helps with physical, financial, mental and social power is **Sarva Bhoga Vashya Mitra**, he may also be called *Sarvato bhogi vashya mitra*; one who helps only with physical and financial power is called **Mahābhoga Vashya Mitra**, he may also be called *Yeketo bhogi vashya mitra*; one who helps with jewels, metals and wood etc is called **Chitra Bhoga Vashya Mitra**, he may also be called *Ubhayato bhogi vashya mitra.*

➤ **Laghu Utthāna Mitra:** The friendship which is for limited period or work is *Laghu Utthāna Mitra.*

➤ **Pitri-Paitāmaha Mitra:** The friendship which has become traditionsl and is coming from many generations is *Pitri Pitāmaha Mitra.*

➤ **Mahat Mitra**: The friendship that lasts for long is *Mahat Mitra.*

➤ **Advaidhya Mitra**: He who is the same in suffering and pleasure; and won't alienate in calamity is called *Advaidhya Mitra.*

While discussing friendship Chānakya raises a question, which has not as yet been satisfactorily answered; some scholars and experienced wise men have remained this side and some that side. The question is:

Kshipram alpo lābhah chirān mahāniti wā. What is good a little gain faster or a delayed but great gain?

The *āchāryas* have given the answer: *Kshipram alpo lābhah karya-desha-samvādakah shreyān.* The wise have answered that a little fast gain is better as the quality and quantity of gain can be known easily.

But Kautilya won't agree with them, as it does not last longer. He says: *Chirād vinipāti beeja sadharmā mahān lābhah shreyā.* That great profit is far greater that takes time from seed to fruit and is safe.

He concludes it with the statement that one must consider the pro-cons, quantitative and qualitative, and calculate well the gain and loss then make a friend:

Yevam dristvā dhruve lābhe lābhānshe cha gunodayam;
Swārtham siddhi paro yāyāt sanhitah sāma- vāyikaih.

14

Mantrimandal: Board of Directors

All the *Mantries*, ministers were both like Directors and Executives. The Mantrimandal has taken the shape of the Board of Directors in the modern age.

After starting or establishing an empire or an organization one must discuss seriously all types of works under hand, and take initiatives of any type only after deep and through discussion: *mantra purvāh sarva ārambhayet*; works are to be started only after deliberations and discussions.

The meeting hall should be completely secure and no one should be allowed to enter without the prior permission of the presiding authority or the Chairman: *tasmānna mantra uddesham ana- āyukto na upagachchhet.*

If the head or presiding authoirity has insulted or deceived a person then he should never take the advice of that person or from his side, i.e. his relatives or friends: *na cha teshām pakshaiyah yeshām apakuryāt.*

Chānakya has laid a lot of stress on the secrecy of the decisions taken in the meetings and has quoted Bhārdwāja also on this point. It has to be kept secret till it is not fully implemented and accomplished. He concludes that chapter with that if the king follows his ways of dealing with the leading members then he is able to protect all the secrets and will come to know of the secrets of others. He should keep his secrets inside as a tortoise keeps his organs inside his body:

One person's ideas should not be accepted. Everything should be discussed directly and indirectly:

> To know the work that is not known as yet;

> To accept or reject the known work;

> If in doubt then to discuss and completely erase all the doubts;

> Partial discussion of one meeting should be discussed completely in another;

Because of the nature of responsibilities, only wise and experienced persons should be on the board of directors or council of ministers: *buddhi vriddhaih sa ārdham āsit mantram.* He gives an example to close that chapter by saying that as a person who knows no scriptures, cannot perform *yagya*, in the same way, a person who has no knowledge of the Shāstras and no experience, can neither give good advice nor can protect secret:

Yathā hya shrotiyah shrāddham na shtām bhoktum arhati;
Yevam ashruta shāstrārtho na mantram shrotum arhati.

Even *Manusmriti*: 7:30; says that tasks can't be accomplished without able administrative and other staff or with unscrupulous, greedy, unwise, and persons infatuated with sensuousness:

So asahāyena moodhena lubdhena akrit buddhinā;
Na shakyo nyāyato netum saktena vishayeshu cha.

The following things should be discussed:

> The way the task is to be started;

> Men and money required;

> Time and place;

> Obstacles and ways to clear the path;

> Accomplishment of task;

The ideas of each person should be heard patiently and none should be insulted: *na kashchid avamanyate sarvasya shrinuyān matam.* One must avoid lengthy discussion: *na deergha kālam mantrayet.*

Kautilya has concluded that after general deliberations on a topic, the Chairman should again discuss the issue with more than one person, three or four before coming to a final decision. He should not follow the advices of only one person: *mantribhih tribhih chaturbhih wā sah manyate.*

The scholars differ on the number of ministers or director in the council or board. Kautilya has mentioned that Manu is in the favour of twelve persons; Brihaspati proposes sixteen; Shukrācharya opts for twenty. Kautilya has the opinion that the number should depend on the available skilled, experienced and able persons: *yathā sāmarthyam iti kautilyah.*

15

Handling Human Resource

Nand dynasty was finished. Maurya dynasty had taken a grand and bright start. Chandragupta Maurya was on the throne. The job of unifying the nation was almost over. Peace and normalcy was returning to the Kingdom. Chānakya wanted to see everything secure. Though he was looking after everything but he was feeling badly the need of a Prime Minister. He was looking for one.

One man from the enemy camp had impressed him as wise, sincere, honest and truthful to the king. He was the famous, rather notorious Amātya Rākshasā, who had earned the nickname of Rākshasā because of his tough stands and very severe punishments. One thing in him that Chānakya appreciated most was the fact that the Amātya did not desert the losing king. He remained true to him and fought for him tooth and nail till the end. He decided to make him the Prime Minister to serve the Mauryan empire.

On the other hand Amātya Rākshasā did not like Chānakya. He hated his guts. He had destroyed a very powerful empire. He was unable to appreciate his direct enemy.

Chānakya met him. He placed some plain cards before him and asked him to be the Prime Minister. Amātya Rākashas blatantly refused.

Intermittently, he kept on persuading him to accept the post and to serve the new empire. He used various means to entice the rigid Amātya who had his prejudices against Chānakya and unable to shake them off.

His secret agents brought some news. Amātya was to attend a function in the residence of a businessman at the most crowded intersection. Chānakya reached there earlier and stopped Amātya Rākshasā. He openly invited him there to become the Prime Minister. He told, "A Prime Minister is not responsible to a king or to a government or to the board of Ministers, he is responsible to the land and the people. The people have a right to see the best person at that high pedestal. You have the ability. People have faith in you. You must accept this challenging job."

Though it seems to be a desperate attempt on the part of Chānakya but it was a calculated step. Amātya Rākshasā was in a fix. He was trapped. After a lot of discussions he accepted the post. It's a rare example when the most important man of the defeated king was made the Prime Minister of the new kingdom.

There is a very famous play entitled "Mudrā Rākashasa" in Samskrit that deals with this central theme.

Appraisal
Getting own men placed in other organization for secret information is as necessary as taking away talented, able, skillful and powerful employees of the competitors for weakening them and strengthening own organization.

Effect

Even in the age of computers and machines the human resource has its immense value as machines are to be handled by men.

Appointment of Executives

The process of appointment and the conditions laid down for each are enough to provide good directives to present day human resource departments all over the world both in government and corporate sectors.

In the present scenario ministers are the legislative heads but in the time of Chānakya ministers were executive heads, definitely of bigger institutions like the modern corporate units. The Mahāmātya was the head of the ministers and chief adviser to the owner, the king or the *Nagar Seth*.

The appointments and duties should be taken as and treated like the appointments and duties of the executives and directors. But the higher the post the appointments were more difficult. The king may work for years without the Mahāmātya but only the fittest person was appointed. Announcements were made and the conditions were declared and the candidates gave the trial. The king or the appointing person appointed one at that high post only when he was fully satisfied that the works at hand and other managements will be smoothly and successfully accomplished by that person. It was open to all. Even persons from other kingdoms were free to try and were appointed when found fit. But the question of faithfulness and sincerity were given supreme preferences.

Salary was not negotiated it was declared along with the powers and duties. There was no question of blackmail on one side and target to be achieved on the other.

Classification of Human Resource

What Kautilya says about the army men is true to employees. Like them the employees also can be divided in various kinds. The classification is done not so much For example:

➤ *Amānit*: Not honoured;

➤ *Nimānita*: Neglected;

➤ *Abhrit*: Unpaid;

➤ *Vyādhita*: Suffering from some disease;

➤ *Navāgat*: Newly appointed;

➤ *Durāyāt*: Belonging to a distant place;

➤ *Prashrānta*: Tired

➤ *Praksheel*: Not skilled;

➤ *Pratihat*: Unsuccessful in life, feeling defeated;

➤ *Hatāgra vega*: Without zeal; one who lacks confidence;

➤ *Anritu prāpta*: Who got no opportunity;

➤ *Āshā Nivedi*: Without hope or faith;

➤ *Parisripta*: Lacks leadership qualities;

➤ *Kalatra grahi*: One who raises finger on others;

➤ *Antah shaiolya*: One who feels and keeps enmity;

➤ *Kupita moola*: Who is angry with the administration;

➤ *Bhinna garbha*: Jealous of colleagues;

➤ *Apasrita*: Harassed by colleagues;

➤ *Atikshipta*: Harassed by insiders and outsiders both;

➤ *Upa nivishta*: Working yet disinterested in the work;

➤ *Samāpta*: Unable to work;

➤ *Upa ruddha*: In problems from one side;

➤ *Pari kshipta*: In problem from many sides;

➤ *Chhinna Dhānya*: One who has no connection with his family;

➤ *Vichhinna purusha vivadha*: Who is unable to foster the family;

➤ *Swa vikshipta*: Working among fully known people;

➤ *Mitra vikshipta*: Working among complete strangers.

16

Money, Wealth and Entrpreneurship

When one is ready to start a new organization or a new project, one must plan it meticulously well, do the leg work, take survey, talk to experts and while doing so one must take the following things into consideration:

> **Shakti**: Ability; skill; know-how; finance; man-power; material; market, etc

> **Place**: Suitability; approach roads; population around; elements required and available;

> **Time**: Suitability of time regarding construction; availability of required things during that season; time for preparation; opening and time of marketing;

> **Problems**: In sight; at present and expected;

> **Expenses**: Inclusives of all expenses; provisions for even unknown expenses;

> **Profit**: Both gross and net;

> **Objections**: From market; dealers; distributors;

> **Future**: The future of project after a decade and also after five decades.

Nowadays, all over the world the people are in a hurry. They forbid others from taking journey without considering the related facts. In his opinion, for smaller works longer journeys can't be under taken. Longer journeys are allowed only when there are substantial and gainful works. One must avoid journey during rain or snow fall. The troubles are then many and works are least accomplished:

> *Sarvām wā hraswa kālāh syuh yātvyāh kārya lāghavāt;*
> *Dererghāh kārya gurutvā dvā varshāvāshah pratra cha.*

Money Begets Money: Artheh Arthāh Prabandhyante

People usually claim that "money begets money" is a western slogan. It is from India, the country of Chārvāka and Chānakya. In the concluding lines of the *Kautilya Arthashāstra*: 9:143:5, there is a shloka that declares that money begets money: **artheh arthāh prabandhyante**; money is managed through money. The meaning is very similar, yet Chānakya is more practical and true in his statement. Actually, money does not come out of money, but more money is earned and managed through money.

Chānakya says: The man who lacks wealth and resources can't accomplish his higher desires despite trying a hundred times. Money is managed by money as the elephants are caught with the help of elephants:

> *Nā dhanāh prāpnuvantya arthāh narā yatna shataih api;*
> *Artheh arthāh prabadhante gajāh prati gajai eva.*

Kshaya, Vyaya Lābha Viparimarsha: Loss, Expense and Profit

The destruction of moveable or immovable property is called loss. The loss of money and other things is called expense. One should start a work when there is no loss and least expense.

One should try to earn such profits which are multifaceted; which can stand the tests of time, place, power, methods, pleasure and pain, victory and defeat; which comes in the present and the flow is to continue in the future also; precious; useful; abundant and extremely good.

Āpatiyān: It generally means objections but in management it means disturbances, to disrupt the working and cause loss and unnecessary heavy expenses. It is caused in four ways through outer agents and inner circle or group in management:

> ➤ It can be caused by outer competitors and personal or organization's enemies and supported by aggrieved or lustful employees;

> ➤ It can be caused by interested employees and supported by outer forces;

> ➤ Caused, ignited and supported by outside elements;

> ➤ Caused and supported solely by employees.

Lābha Vighna: Obstacles in Profit

There are many things that work as obstacles and hurdles in the way of earning, income and profit: sensuousness; anger; kindness; shyness; deception; backbiting; ego; compassion; godly fear; moral fear; pride; unrighteousness; neglect; ill-behaviour; doubt; lack of faith; friendly with enemy; seasons and natural causes.

Artha Anartha Sanshaya Yuktāh: Classification into Good and Bad Wealth

According to earning and spending the wealth is classified in many divisions which include even the obstacles, and Kautilya suggests that one should try to clear the obstacles first: *Tasyām purvām purvām-prakriti nām-anartha mokshayitum yatet.* After discussing a few artha and anartha, he has discussed *Artha-Trivarga,* wealth triangle; *Anartha Trivarga,* bad wealth triangle and *Sanshaya Trivarga,* obstacle triangles. If the obstacles are from the relatives like son, brother and other relatives then one should use *sāma* and *danda* to pacify it but if it is from general public then one should use *danda* and *bheda* but if it is from officials then *dāna* and *bheda* should be used to pacify them and clear the obstacles. It is called *Anuloma* if these ways are followed if otherwise then it is called *Prati Loma*, and if mixed ways are followed then it is called *Vyāmishra*.

> **Āpadartha**: The wealth that is lost because of negligence; forced to return after earning it; or causes extrenuous expenses is *Āpadartha Artha*.

> **Sanshaya roopa**: The wealth that is used to create doubt and instigate infight between a competitor and his friend or friemds is *Sanshaya roopa*.

> **Arthānubandha Artha**: The wealth spent to uproot the enemy and create friendly relations with his friends is *Arthānubandha Artha*.

> **Nir-anubandha Artha**: The wealth taken to help a disinterested party is *Nir-anubandha artha*.

> **Artha anubandha anartha**: The wealth spent on helping the competitors of own competitor is *Artha anubandha anartha*, bad or useless wealth.

> **Samantatah Arth Āpata**: When suddenly the income starts coming from all the four directions then it is called *Samantatah artha āpata*.

> **Artha Sanshaya āpata**: If doubts and obstacles are created in the above wealth coming from all the four directions then it is called *Artha sanshaya āpata*.

Income and Profit

According to Kautilya the Income/ Profit can be divided in groups:

> *Ādeya*: That which comes very easily; saved easily and none can snatch it away easily;

> *Pratādeya*: It is just opposite to the first one. Some profits are earned the hard way. The person or organization that depends on such income or profit is easily destroyed.

> *Prasādaka*: The profit that gives pleasure to family, relatives, friends and strangers also.

> *Prakopaka*: The opposite of *Prasādaka* is called prakopaka. It gives pain to all.

> *Hrasvakāla*: The profit that comes with little labour and small investment.

> *Tanukashya*: The profit that one gets after working only a bit, only for show.

> *Alpa vyaya*: The profit that one gets after spending only food and lodging.

> *Mahān*: The higher profit that one gets very fast.

> *Viddha udaya*: The profit that is to come in future is *vriddha udaya*.

> *Kalpa*: The profit in which there is no known problem is called *Kalpa*.

> *Dharmya*: The income that is earned righteously.

> *Puroga*: The gifts that one gets unconditionally.

He goes on discussing the problems that can arise out of income, earning and profit. The connotations of harassment and obstacles to trade may have changed. However, the fact that anti-dumping measures exist or that cartelization has to be coped with or adverse terms of trade have to be accounted for in certain sectors underscore that safeguards are essential even in current times and those responsible for managing these measures should be responsible.

Furthermore, Kautilya was cognizant of the fact that the terms of trade were not just dependent on the economics but also on other various parameters. The traders had to keep in mind the political or strategic advantages in exporting or importing from a particular country. The proliferation of free trade agreements in recent times underscores this point because there is a definite political dimension to trade treaties and agreements.

Scams and Punishment

While discussing Scams and Punishment described in Kautilya *Arthashāstra*; the incident of lamp must be reminded to the readers to refresh their memory and concept what honesty and sincerity was for Chānakya, and how sincerely he saved the royal treasure. It was his righteous approach that all else were afraid of doing anything wrong out of the fear of known and unknown punishment that Chānakya pronounced.

Vaidehaka Rakshanam: Saving the People

All the thirteen chapters of this *Adhikaran* named *Kantakshodhan*, saving the people; deals with different excesses and crimes committed against the mass and adequate punishment for every crime. It is solely dedicated to saving the mass from different types of persons and crimals including the government officials. It shows ways of saving the people from and related punishment towards the culprits. It's not only the duty and responsibility of only the ruler or the administration but it's the duty and responsibility of each individual to save the self, family and society against the following:

> - **Professionals** from washer man to mason and from sculptor to goldsmith and from doctors to actors;
> - **Traders** and **businessmen** from weight and measurement to rates; from deception to non-ordered articles; hoarding to mixing and from interest to freight;
> - **Natural disasters** like fire, flood, contagious diseases, famine, rats, dangerous animals, demons etc.
> - **Conspirators**: local or from other places;
> - **Immoral** and **disguised** persons;
> - **Suspicious characters**;
> - **Murderers** and **absconders**;
> - **Government officials** and **workers**;

- Thieves, robbers and cheats;
- Tāntriks
- Rapists and immoralists;

Chānakya is very severe towards rapists with strong punishments. If one rapes a minor girl of his own caste his **hands should be chopped up**; if one rapes a mature girl his **index and middle fingers be cut off** and two hundred panas for the girl; if one rapes a girl whose engagements has already taken place then his **hands should be cut off** and a fine of 400 panas be levied.

The climax is that if the king has wrongfully punished anyone and the amount has already been deposited in the treasure then the people have the right to ask the king to pay the innocent person thirty times greater amount in lieu there of. That amount should be first put in some reservoir then distributed among the brāhmins:

Adanya dandene rāgyo dandah trishad gunoh ambhasi;
Varunāya pradātvyo brāhmanebhyah statah param.

17

Crushing Rebellion

One very important aspect of good governance and success in any field depends on correct and timely gathering and sending messages and orders. It is essential also for success in battles and in crushing rebellion. Chānakya worked out a nice way of signaling and passing on information, messages and orders through light-signaling. Such signaling was in vogue in India. Chānakya improved it.

The height of this lighting system was given perfect shape from the capital city Pātliputra to the north of River Gangā by connecting the palace at Kumbharār with the palace in Vaishali to another at Kesariya; from there to Nandan Garh Lauriā with the last one Chānaki Garh. Whatever message was sent through light from the Royal palace was received at all other centres which were reciprocated from there. The palace at Kubhrār was demolished and the system jeopardized. Yet among the remaining palaces the system worked. It continued till the Moghul period. But somehow, the British did not like it and the signaling was stopped though they experimented from Gola Ghar to other places successfully.

A very important thing that Kautilya says related to shifting of loyalty of an employee towards the competitors: it is the duty of both the immediate boss and supreme to stop shifting of loyalty of any employee, higher and lower, irrespective of rank and salary, towards the competitors. Kautilya has used the words king and enemy:

Yevam swa vishaye kritya- unkrityah cha vichakshanah;
Par- upajātpāt sanrakshet pradhānān kshudrakān api.

Distracters: Problem Mongers

As usual and as in the past the money is earned by many people uncluding the labourers, farmers, professional and employees but basically and truly controlled by the governments and businessmen; earlier by kings and Vaishyas. In Indian concept all those who are in business, are Vaishyas. In modern and European concept the business people are divided in different categories and business world in different worlds from traders to corporate world. Despite the divisions they are all businessmen, the Vaishyas. The meaning of businessman is very flat and clear. Kautilya searches out and declares that in the management of a kingdom so in the management of business and industries, there were (and there are) different distracters. Chānakya divides them in different categories and shows the ways to win them over.

People's Behaviour and luring them

Kautilya has described certain behaviours of people who can be won over in case of need. There are four behaviours that he feels which make a man seducible. They are: anger, fright, greed, and pride. The moot point here is why these four only? Many of "Kautilya's" teachings and policies are influenced by the teachings of "Vedas", which tell us that a human being is made up of mind, body and intellect (brain). Out of these the body acts either at the command of the mind or at the instance of intellect. Intellect is defined as the capacity to control mind and comes from study and reflection. Mind is a collection of our feelings, emotions, thoughts, etc. While intellect rationalizes, mind tells the emotion.

Further, mind exhibits three characteristics: it is insatiable, it wanders even faster than the speed of light, and it gets attached. All these things make one dependent on the world. A person feels stress when his mind rules over his intellect. This is the state of unfulfilled desires. Desires create mental weaknesses, whereas when intellect rules over the mind the desires become aims and ambitions.

There are emotions and trend that have been responsible for the ruin of persons, families, societies, business houses, corporate and kingdoms. One must control them because both fulfilled and unfulfilled desires could lead one to different states and create:

> ➤ **Sex:** The desire of sensuous pleasure is the greatest distracter. It is life and life creating if it is under control and one indulges in sex only with his/ her legally wedded spouse but it ruins if one fails to control it.

> **Anger**: Mind experiences anger which is an obstruction to what one desires.

> **Greed**: When the craving or the desire becomes very strong it becomes greed. Greedy persons are always despised. This further leads to arrogance which with passage of time, becomes envy.

> **Envy**: Envy is created by others' success and happiness. Anyone can be envious of anyone else. Envy gives a sense of failure and insecurity which leads to fear.

> **Fear**: The feeling that many things will remain unaccomplished in this life creates fear. There is also the fear of losing what one has already accumulated or what is already in possession.

> **Moha**: Moha, attachment, is the other state that Vedas and other Scriptures talk about. It surfaces with too much of attachment with persons, places, things or achievements. But Kautilya lays stress on pride as the fourth seducible element in a man that relates to arrogance. When working one must identify oneself with the work but one should not expect its fruit. One must be detached from the outcome. The duties are to be completed the results are not to be waited for.

These are very common weaknesses. One faces people with these trends: one or many in one. The problem is how to identify these people and how to control them. Kautilya has an answer for this and shows the way.

The Group of Enraged

Anger is exhibited when one's desires are obstructed.

> One who is cheated/denied after being promised certain rewards (increment in pay, status, etc).

> The one of two or more persons, who is equally competent but is humiliated because the other is

assigned a job requiring those competencies that the other one also possesses.

➤ One who is in disfavour because of a favoruite of his superior.

➤ One who is unable to deliver results on account of being challenged to a particular assignment. This will particularly happen in the organizations, which have a focus just on the results and not on the efforts that a person puts.

➤ One who is distressed after being transferred to a far-flung area, or an area of his dislike. Here one possibility is that a person is willing to take on the transfer but is not remunerated properly, and another possibility is that the person is not willing to take on such a transfer but is forced to do so.

➤ One who is on an assignment not by his choice and not of his choice. That is, being put on an assignment without even being motivated for it. It could be something, which is away from the promised career path of an employee; something that definitely adds value to the organization but not to the employee as such (as perceived by the employee); quite true in case of knowledge workers.

➤ One who has not achieved his objective in the organization even after trying hard and giving his best. This could be because of a fault in the culture of that organization. For example, at times we see that even after being trained for a purpose the employee is not able to add enough to his function – the answer could lie with the fact that the employee hasn't learnt much, his fault. But what concerns us here is that even though willingness is there to perform but the culture hinders that performance.

- One who is hindered from doing his duty; maybe because of paucity of time, or because responsibility given is not complemented with required authority.

- One whose remuneration, financial and non-financial is incommensurate with the efforts he puts in. One deserving but deprived of an office he aspires. This could especially happen if there is delayed or no promotion (job enrichment), and/or delayed or no inter-functional or to that extent even intra-functional movement, job enlargement.

- One held back by his peers or superiors in an organization for their own interests.

- One who is reprimanded and/or punished, whether such reprimand/ punishment is justified or not, after serving the organization loyally.

- One prevented from indulging in conduct, not in conformance to the organization's code of Conduct.

- One, the credit of whose work is stolen by others.

To Lure the Enraged

Reinforce perceptions that such people hold about their organization by telling them, how their organization and managers lack the eye of knowledge, commonsense and also the experience to see what one is worth. Also explain to them the "detrimental effects" that such behaviour of their organization and managers can have on the organization. Invite them then to join another organization to realize their potential.

The Group of Frightened

Those who have the fear of losing something:

- One who has thwarted someone, that is, one who has pushed himself up by pulling others down.

- One who has committed a serious mistake; a deliberate act detrimental to the organization.

- One who has become known for a wrong act. This act might be done in a personal capacity and not a professional one.

- One frightened by the punishment meted out to another for a like offence.

- One who has seized someone else's work/credit.

- One who is subdued by authority.

- One who has suddenly amassed a lot of wealth at the expense of the organization.

- One disliked by his superiors.

- One who entertains hostility towards superiors or the organization itself.

To Lure the Frightened

These people already have a sense of insecurity. Reinforce this sentiment by warning them of a possible "harm" that they stand from their organization due to its own (incorrect) apprehension of being harmed from them. Show them a safer haven where they can grow.

The Group of Greedy

State of overwhelming desires.

- One who is impoverished for money/respect/opportunities. Such people want to grow really fast in their organizations.

- One in a calamity. Calamity generated out of one's own recurring actions.

- One indulging in vices. Again, this could be both personal and professional.

> One indulging in rash transactions. Rashness of transactions apparently involves a financial loss or expectation of a great gain. Such a fellow will accept challenges rashly - without even thinking whether they are achievable or not, greedy of being noticed.

> A person who believes in personal gain by withholding information.

To Lure the Greedy

Reinforce their desire by amplifying the fact that their organization rewards those who are devoid of spirit, intelligence, and eloquence, but not those endowed with qualities of the self, reinforce the "fact" that our organization has a culture of acknowledging and rewarding persons of distinction, join us.

The Group of Proud

Relates to arrogance that follows greed.

> One who is filled with self-conceit, self-importance, pride, vanity, snobbery, arrogance;

> One desirous of honor.

> One resentful of the honor done to a colleague, who is perceived a competitor or rival.

> One placed in a low position, but is convinced that he is capable of being at a higher position in the hierarchy.

> One fiery in temper.

> One given to violence (physical, verbal or non verbal in nature).

> One dissatisfied with his emoluments i.e. one who thinks that he is getting much less than what he deserves.

Now that we have identified such people who can be targeted for the purpose of head hunting, following is the manner prescribed by Kautilya to approach them.

To Lure the Proud

These people need to get their ego massaged. Approach them by impressing upon them that their organization is fit for and is of benefit to only people with lower qualities and people of little or no intelligence or conviction or abilities; not for people of their standing. Invite them to join an organization that "knows" how to honor persons of distinction, come to us. Professionals with years of experience can build on the knowledge provided and use it to their good. It however goes without saying that a lot of networking is required to identify such people who display the behaviors described above.

Deal with them and be safe and secure. Allow these emotions to grow or leave such people free then get ruined completely in no time at all. The reasons for the ruins of empires and the rich have been one or two or many of these emotions and trends.

18

Departments and Officers: Then and Now

Chānakya had thought over division of labour and division of departments; the heads of those departments and divisions from sectional head to executive head but the king was the overall head. He had created *Adhikāri, Adhyaksha, Pada* and *Upa-pada* and also *Padādhikāri* as given below. He has used other words also. In this book, the use of those words have been deliberately avoided to maintain the flow and rhythm of both writing and reading. But these words are important for those who wish to know them and also for those who may like to compare with the words in modern use. So, some of the important words are being given below:

Ankayamit	Stamped letter
Ankeshit Lekhā	Audited account
Anga Rakshaka	Bodyguard
Antaranga Sachiva	Private secretary
Antah Vānijya	Internal trade
Anshadhar	Shareholder
Aksha Patal	The head of income and expenditure
Aksha Patal Adhyaksha	Accountant general
Aksha Shālā	Gold testing centre
Adhikartā or Sanchālaka	Director
Adhikarmi	Overseer

Adhikāri	Officer
Adhikshaka	Superintendent
Adhishthātā	Presiding officer
Agradāya Dhana	Advanced money
Agrasar	Forward
Aticharana	Transgression
Adyā Vadhika	Up-to-date
Adhikartā	Director
Adhikarmi	Overseer
Adhikār Patra	Charter
Adhikāri	Officer
Adhikosha	Bank
Adhigrahana	Acquisition
Anugypti	License
Anudesha	Instructions
Anupuraka	Supplementary
Anurakshak	Escort
Anuvesha Patra	Visa
Antapāl	In-charge of borders
Abhikartā	Agent
Abhiyantā	Engineer
Abhirakshak	Custodian
Abhilekhapāl	Keeper of records
Aparideya	Non-transferable
Apa Lābha	Profiteering
Apratibhāvya	Non-bailable
Apratyādeya	Irrecoverable
Avadhānaka	Caretaker
Abhigyān	Identification
Abhigya Patra	Identity card
Abhinirnaya	Verdict
Abhinyāsa	Layout
Abhibhāvak	Guardian
Abhiyantā	Engineer
Abhiyoktā	Complainant

Abhiyoga	Accusation
Abhivaktā	Pleaser
Abhirakshak	Custodian
Abhilekha	Record
Ābkāri Adhikāri	Excise officer
Abhakti	Disloyalty
Āyakar Adhikāri	Income tax officer
Uccha Adhikāri	High command
Upa Mukhya	Deputy chief
Karanika	Clerk
Karanika Pradhān	Head clerk
Karanika Mukhya	Chief clerk
Kar Nirdhāraka	Assessor
Karna Pāla	Quarter master
Karmakār	Workman
Kārāgārika	Jailor
Kārmika	Statistical officer
Kārya Nāyaka	Charge de Affairs
Kāryabhāri	Incharge
Kārya Vāhaka	Acting
Khanda Nirikshaka	Block inspector
Gana	Organization; Council
Ganaka/ Gānanika	Accountant
Ganikādhyaksha	Prostitute controller
Grihapati	Warden
Grāmanika	Village head
Griha Rakshaka	Home guard
Granthagārika	Librarian
Grām Gāmanika	Chief of a village
Chālaka	Driver
Dandapāla	Commander
Dandādhisha	Magistrate
Duta	Messenger
Dāti	Delivery
Dhāraka	Keeper

Dhātri	Midwife
Dhvajapati	Flag officer
Nagarpāla	City father
Nagar Rakshaka	Civil guard
Nāyaka	Captain
Nidarshan	Direction
Nibandhaka	Registrar
Niyantraka	Controller
Nirikashaka	Inspector
Nivi	Net income
Nibandhaka	Accounts clerk
Naubalādhyaksha	Navy officer
Pattanpati	Harbor master
Parichar	Attendant
Parichālaka	Operator
Paryavekshaka	Supervisor
Paur Mukhya	City magistrate
Prabandhaka	Manager
Prāntapati	Governor
Pritanāpati	Brigadier
Bhāndāgār	Godown
Bhārika	Porter
Bhriti	Wage
Mantranā	Council
Sangha	Federation
Senā pati	Commander-in-Chief
Senā nāyaka	Commander

आत्म–विकास/व्यक्तित्व विकास

Also Available
in Hindi

Also Available
in Hindi

Also Available
in Kannada, Tamil

Also Available
in Kannada

Also Available
in Kannada

हमारी सभी पुस्तकें www.vspublishers.com पर उपलब्ध हैं

Also Available
in Hindi, Kannada

Also Available
in Hindi, Kannada

www.ingramcontent.com/pod-product-compliance
Lightning Source LLC
Chambersburg PA
CBHW071754090426
42737CB00012B/1819